Washington Gladden, Ohio Columbus Barber, James McGee, George Gunton

Debate on Trusts, Between O.C. Barber and Hon. J.A. Kohler

also the debate on trusts between Dr. Washington Gladden, of Columbus, Ohio,

and George Gunton of New York City, at the Chautauqua Assembly, August 26,

1889

Washington Gladden, Ohio Columbus Barber, James McGee, George Gunton

Debate on Trusts, Between O.C. Barber and Hon. J.A. Kohler
also the debate on trusts between Dr. Washington Gladden, of Columbus, Ohio, and George Gunton of New York City, at the Chautauqua Assembly, August 26, 1889

ISBN/EAN: 9783337735456

Printed in Europe, USA, Canada, Australia, Japan

Cover: Foto ©Suzi / pixelio.de

More available books at **www.hansebooks.com**

DEBATE ON TRUSTS,

BETWEEN

O. C. BARBER

AND

HON. J. A. KOHLER,

Ex-Member of the General Assembly, and Ex-Attorney-General of the State of Ohio.

———————

ALSO THE

DEBATE ON TRUSTS

BETWEEN

DR. WASHINGTON GLADDEN,
Of Columbus, Ohio.

AND

GEORGE GUNTON,
Of New York City.

At the Chautauqua Assembly, August 26, 1889.

With other Interesting Articles on the same Subject by Men of Note.

———————

AKRON:
BEACON PUB. CO., Printers.
1889, .

PREFACE.

In publishing this debate in pamphlet form, for distribution, I am prompted in part by selfishness. Being largely interested in corporations that are made up of different companies and corporations, their plants and franchises being merged in one corporation with a view to the profit incident to such organizations, I am very anxious that they be better understood. They are now and have been made the target for severe criticism, and unfriendly legislation has been suggested and urged against them by the press and by public speakers who are entirely in ignorance of their operations and purposes. My opinion is that Captain Kohler, having had experience both as a legislator and Attorney-General of the State, has as ably, perhaps, presented his side of the case as any one could. It would have been better for both parties to have omitted the personalities of the debate, which no doubt have very much offended the good taste of Mr. and Mrs. Straightlace and Mr. and Mrs. Goodsoul, yet they will please bear in mind that they are not the only ones to be considered. The human family has diverse feelings, and very many think such personalities as we have indulged in have only added zest to the argument and brought out more clearly the points that each has made.

In debating this question I have made no attempt to define a trust, but the debate has developed that it is a combination under a new form—an association for commercial purposes. In the corporations that I am interested in, we have adopted a legal form of combination. Trusts vary from corporations in this one point—there are no statutes thus far that regulate them or charter them. Perhaps those who have adopted them see some advantages because of the absence of restraints which give them greater freedom in their operations.

It is not so clear that the trust form of combination is better than the corporate form of combination, either for the public or for those interested; but it is very clear that association and combination are features in commerce absolutely necessary to an extended business. In the wonderful development of the resources of this country, which are calling for the use of every dollar of capital of the country, together with every man, woman and child that wishes to work for an honest living, new methods are constantly being suggested to facilitate development and commerce. It has not occurred to all that this industrial activity which in this century has brought into use forty-six million horsepower by the discovery of the use of steam, representing the working force of a billion of men, is immensely cheapening both the products of the soil and factory, and that each individual laborer's power of production is largely increased by these improved methods of production. This being the case, it often occurs that the markets are glutted with what is called over-production, and then follows a state of inactivity consequent on such over-production, and the distress of those who have not had the ability to provide for themselves a sufficient surplus in time of activity to carry them over the period of inactivity. Would it not be as well for the people, if the waste of over-production were checked and these periods of extraordinary activity toned down a little and the period of inactivity toned up a little?

The mission of association, co-operation, or combination, in whatever form it may take, either that of a trust or corporation, is to systematize commerce and manufacturing—to prevent waste of over-production and distribution and to perfect the processes of production and methods of distribution. In whatsoever particular branch of business they do this, then they take that branch of business out of the general chaos, and if by these methods they can keep only the given number of people necessary to supply the want of the particular branch steadily employed, they have accomplished one good to mankind, even though it savors of monopoly. Monopoly does not always mean despotism, but it sometimes means superior methods and ability to serve the public in the line monopolized. Up jumps the little grumbler now, and asks, What is to become of the surplus people, after all branches of business have been systematized? My answer is, that there will be no surplus people. Either man will find it unnecessary to work as many hours per day, or he will have more wants to be supplied. There can never be an over-production of comfortable and pleasant homes, and the cheaper they become, the more abundant they will be.

The United States is using nearly one-sixth of the steam power of the world. With a population of sixty millions of people she is using a steam force equal to one hundred and sixty-six millions' able bodied men, and if we have a population of three people to one able bodied man, this steam force represents, in an operative sense, a population of five hundred millions of people. If by some terrible catastrophe the steam force of the world should be suddenly wiped out of existence, what, think you, man would do? How many hours would he have to work to maintain his present wants? And yet it has not been 100 years since its usefulness was first developed. And there is not a single horse-power of steam that does not imply association, co-operation, combination, trust, or corporation. The latter are the masters of this very good servant of man.

What a sad commentary on our present civilization that a great government like that of the United States should abandon the use of steam printing at the behest of a few disgruntled printers! Every member of Congress and Senator of the United States that voted to abandon the steam press in the Bureau of Engraving and Printing is open to severe criticism.

The Philadelphia Record truthfully says, "Such a victory of retrogression is more harmful to the cause of honest labor than many defeats could be. This is pre-eminently the age of machinery, and it is an error to suppose that the recurrence of the Bureau of Engraving and Printing to antiquated methods of production is an advantage either to working-men or to the government."

This is not only an age of machinery, but it is an age of organization, co-operation, and improved business methods for handling the wonderful discoveries that are daily being unfolded to us. Besides steam, we have electricity and the many thousand labor-saving machines that have multiplied man's ability to care for himself.

In reading over my opponent's letters, it strikes me that he has had a Rip Van Winkle sleep or that he was thinking of the good old times of Lord Coke, when he penned the following: "The evil results of such immense concentration of capital and enterprise are not entirely of a pecuniary character. The question is broader. The time is coming, if it has not already come, when we will not measure everything in this world by the dollar-and-cent standard. 'Is not life more than meat, and the body more than raiment?'" [How pathetic!] "Time was when a young man, active, eager and energetic, and having a capital of a few hundred dollars, found the door of opportunity open. All the avenues of trade and manufacturing were broad streets, with no barriers across them. Competition was open and free and a young man could safely embark his small earnings or his inheritance and work his way to the front as a manufacturer and business man. There was little risk ; his success depended mainly upon his own efforts."

Those must have been the good old times referred to some 300 years ago, when Lord Coke kept competition open, or a period when there was no competition, if it were possible for every young man to work himself forward to success; but in this day, such sophistry to a young man of energy looks just a little fishy and sickening.

There are more successes to-day and greater possibilities of success than in any other period of the world's history. The young are succeeding to the well-established business of the old, and the old are retiring and turning over their business to the improved methods of the young, and each successive generation finds superior advantages over the preceding ones, or else civilization is coming to a halt. My opponent in this debate has made some wonderfully incorrect statements and specifications, which I have not undertaken to answer. I have confined myself, as far as he would permit me, to general principles, and have only deviated from the same except in matters with which I am familiar. He has criticised me severely for quoting so much as I have from eminent authorities. I have done so in every instance for the reason that the substance quoted had a bearing on the question we were discussing, and for the reason that they have stated the matter better than I could possibly state it myself. But such a criticism from an attorney seems rather absurd to a layman. What little knowledge I have of the methods of lawyers, I have noticed that in presenting a case to a jury or a judge, they generally have before them standard authorities on the subjects they are talking about, and read and quote from the same copiously.

Mr. Kohler, in his letter No. 4, says: "In this connection, I may refer to the strawboard business ; such reports are not always true, and if there is any error in this statement I would be glad to be corrected." And then he goes on and makes ridiculous statements about the profits of the strawboard business and the management, and draws unjust conclusions. He has done the same thing in the match business, and when his attention was called to the unjust statements he had made about the match business, he "jumped onto me," to use a slang phrase, with "both feet" and re-asserted his figures in a new form, showing his utter ignorance of the question he was discussing. I show in my last letter, I think to the satisfaction of all, that he did not know what he was talking about. If his statements about other trusts and combinations that he has held up to public contempt are founded on no better evidence or knowledge of facts, and I dare say they are not, his little arguments and long-drawn and ridiculous conclusions can have little weight with a careful reader. There will be found in the latter part of this pamphlet an article clipped from the *American Economist* on the subject of the Sugar Trust, which very fully shows up how false his statements on that subject were. To me it seems that he has drawn his inspirations and misinformation from the common stock in trade of the political agitator and newspaper reports, which are often garbled for political reasons.

Other interesting papers containing much information and the debate of Dr. Gladden and Mr. Gunton will be found following our debate.

I submit the papers to the public for their consideration.

O. C. BARBER.

AKRON, OHIO, October 26, 1889.

DISCUSSION ON TRUSTS.

No. 1.

Mr. Barber to Mr. Kohler.

PROPOSITION FOR A JOINT DISCUSSION ON TRUSTS.

WEDNESDAY, May 8, 1889.

Hon. J. A. Kohler.

DEAR SIR : Some ten days since, as I was leaving for the West,
I bought a *Beacon*, and one of the first items that attracted my attention was the following Peninsula correspondence :

Hon. J. A. Kohler, of Akron, delivered a very excellent address on the
comparison and contrast of times and customs of our country as compared with
foreign nations. He drew some very good lessons that bear very hard on trusts
and monopolies, which are the curse of this country to-day. It would be well
to have addresses of this kind delivered all over this country, in every village
and hamlet. It was a fair, unprejudiced argument, irrespective of Democratic
or Republican ties. These are the kind of speeches we need to enlighten our
voters. As long as the parties will send out speakers who speak for party and
not for principle or the good of country we can expect to have trusts, &c., unless they make that an issue.   A. O. I.

It has furnished me food for considerable thought since, and I
have concluded to address you this open letter.

The question of trade combinations and trusts is frequently
referred to by public speakers. On general principles, I believe
such combinations and trusts are a benefit to the public. What you
may have said on the occasion referred to above, I dare say, made
some impression on the few people that you addressed ; but, in comparison, the short paragraph of the reporter talked to a multitude,
while you only addressed such a congregation as could assemble in
a small hall or church. The reporter, "A O. I.," seems to think
you have some good thoughts bearing on trusts and monopolies that
should be heard in every hamlet. Now, as I am a believer in combinations made for legitimate purposes, and as I belong to companies that are erroneously styled trusts and monopolies, and know
them to be good instead of bad in their effect, both on the general
public and those interested, I dislike very much to see such companies or organizations held up to public contempt without having

a chance to talk back. I fully realize, in addressing you on this subject, that I am, to a large extent, bucking against public opinion, and that I am also at a disadvantage in debating with a person who has had long experience in public affairs, and is schooled in debate, while my education has better qualified me to cope with material things than to do battle with words ; yet, if you will accept the challenge, I will try and make myself understood. I would like to hear what so great a teacher may have to say on this subject.

Will you please address me a letter, stating your objections to trusts and trade combinations, giving your opinion in full as to the effect on the public.   If you will do so, I will present the opposite side of the question to the best of my ability, and the two papers can be published together, either by the courtesy of the *Beacon* or some other paper, or at my expense on a sheet which will be for free distribution.   In addressing you this letter, I do so with the kindest of feelings, and with respect to your ability, and with only one purpose in view, viz, that the public may profit by your teachings, if they are correct ; or, that the companies that I am interested in may not be held up to public contempt.   I hope, in considering the subject, you will define the difference between labor combinations (which should also include combinations among professional men to maintain certain fees for their work) and commercial combinations.   Please let us go into the subject quite fully, if at all.

Very truly yours,   O. C. BARBER.

[The *Beacon* gladly opens its columns to the discussion Mr. Barber proposes, and if his proposition is accepted by Mr. Kohler, an intensely interesting and profitable interchange of views on a very live and important question may be looked for.—*Editor Beacon.*]

No. 1.

Mr. Kohler in Reply to Mr. Barber's No. 1.

THE CHALLENGE ACCEPTED AND THE TRUST DISCUSSION TO GO ON.

FRIDAY, May 10, 1889.

O. C. Barber, Esq.

DEAR SIR : Referring to your letter to me, published in the *Beacon* Wednesday, I find that the report of my remarks at Peninsula has furnished you "food for considerable thought." I am glad of this, but assure you that I make no claim whatever to the title of great teacher which you generously concede to me. Quoting further from your letter, you say (speaking classically) that you "fully realize that you are bucking against public opinion." If this is so, then allow me to suggest that there is nothing for me to do or say. Inasmuch as the public is already fully advised and judgment formed against your side, as lawyers say, the onus or burden of proof is on you. It does not matter much what my opinion may be. It is the public you want to convince that trade combinations or trusts, as they are called, are really useful in design and operation. I have no more interest in the matter of trusts than any other citizen, and am not putting myself forward specially as an antagonist of trusts, or as a champion of public interests.

I claim the right to speak plainly and freely upon public questions, whenever called upon to do so. This I did at Peninsula, at a meeting which I was invited to address, and in my remarks I spoke of the growth and consolidation of corporate interests and the combination and concentration of capital and vast business interests by a method of organization commonly called a trust. I expressed the opinion then, as I do now, that such combinations, pooling arrangements or trusts, or whatever you may call them, were contrary to sound policy and opposed to the best interests of the country; and you say that public opinion is in accord with this view. Now, I am perfectly willing to give my reasons for the view I have expressed, and will gladly discuss the question with you. But with all due respect, I claim that you should write the letter, giving your reasons why these institutions and agencies are good and not bad in their effects. I would prefer meeting the question in orderly oral discussion, face to face, if this were possible; but as you prefer the columns of a newspaper, if you will write the letter, showing wherein and how such trusts and trade combinations benefit the public, I will, without delay, consider and fairly evdeavor to meet your arguments.

The question is one of great importance, and for one I would be very glad indeed to hear your side. Very few people know exactly what trusts are. The creation and management of them are generally close and confidential matters. You have had large experience and success in directing affairs of that kind and have advantages and opportunities of enlightening the public that I do not possess. Now, understand that I accept your proposal with the fullest confidence in your sincerity and earnestness in this matter. But as you are the challenging party, I await your letter.

        Respectfully yours,
                            J. A. KOHLER.

No. 2.

Mr. Barber in Reply to Mr. Kohler's No. 1.

FIRST PAPER IN THE DISCUSSION ON TRUSTS.

SATURDAY, May 18, 1889.

Hon. J. A. Kohler.

DEAR SIR : On my return home my attention was called to your letter of the 10th inst. in the *Beacon*. I have to say in reply that I shall not haggle with you over the point as to who should commence the debate or write the first letter on the subject we wish to discuss ; but before going on with the debate, I wish to suggest that hereafter when you quote anything I have written, you do so correctly and not misquote my words and make a text of the same for erroneous conclusions. I did not say, as you quote me, viz, "Fully realize that you are bucking against public opinion." What I did say, was that I fully realized that to some extent I was bucking against public opinion. You use this language in part, call it classical, and draw the erroneous conclusion that I have acknowledged that the public, to use your own language, "is already fully advised, and judgment formed against your side." Therefore you conclude, "speaking classically," as a lawyer should, "that the onus, or burden of proof, is on you." Inasmuch as you have put in your demurrer, and have come to the conclusion that there is nothing for you to do or say—which, by the way, I had more than half mistrusted—I will proceed with my case, after one more side remark. I shall not, judging from my past experience, always speak classically, and may not always use the best English. Neither will I refrain, if it suits my convenience, from using a slang word now and then. My time is too thoroughly taken up with business affairs to be too particular on these points. What I hope to do is to show that combinations of capital in the pursuit of any enterprise of whatever kind, when for legitimate purposes, are perfectly proper, whether such combinations start from a beginning with only a cash capital to accomplish the result, or whether an aggregation of capital invested in an enterprise, but owned by different people or corporations, be consolidated in one combination or trust.

It is no new principle that in union there is strength. The first trust formed in this country was the trust of the Colonies, formed for self-preservation. This trust brought about and conducted the war of the Revolution for our National Independence. They did well and built wisely. True, there were defects in organization, and while their declaration of principles was correct in the main, yet human weakness, under this trust, permitted a great wrong—that of human slavery. Have they not paid the penalty of that wrong? So will every trust pay the penalty of its mistakes. Laws more subtile than those formulated by legislatures are constantly at work correcting wrongs.

The basis of all commercial transactions is profit. Would it be wise to reverse the order of things by law, and make the basis of all such transactions loss? Or to obstruct commerce by legislation that would bring about such a result? Organization in business is as necessary for profit as organization in politics is to success. Neither is it anything new for two or more people to organize themselves together for business purposes. It is true that of late it has been on a larger scale than in the good old times past, but in those good old times we had no steam, electricity, etc., etc. What one man could build a railway from New York to Chicago? I doubt, could a man live with his full strength to be a thousand years old, if he could half finish the task. It is absolutely imperative for people to associate themselves together in order to accomplish any grand result; hence these large trusts and combinations. They are successfully being formed for commercial and manufacturing enterprises and for religious and political purposes. They prevent waste, and facilitate distribution; create moral sentiment and control the state. The more complete the organization the greater the result for good or bad.

What a lonely creature one human being, if left alone on this earth, would be. He might have all the wisdom known to man, and yet he would soon succumb to his environment, and would associate with the beasts of the field, and before the end of his days, might bellow like a calf. But in a multitude there is strength by association. The more good workers you can associate with you for a given result, the grander your success. The more capital you can control, the greater the magnitude of your undertakings.

After all, Mr. Kohler, where would you put the limit on the efforts of man or men? Do you want to say that there shall be no combination of capital and talent, and that each man shall work out his own existence in his own line of thought, without association with his neighbors? I am told by the manufacturers of reapers and mowers, that, owing to the army of agents they employ and the competition among manufacturers of these articles, it costs about as much to sell a reaper as it does to make one. Now, suppose that they form a trust, make a pool where their interests are common

and make a saving of 75 per cent. in selling their product, giving a
part of the saving to the farmer, a part to labor, and keeping a portion themselves ?   Who would be harmed by the combination, even
though the promoters thereof accumulate a fortune ?   It is a well
demonstrated fact that the result of combinations for manufacturing purposes has been to reduce the price of the article manufactured to the public, and the cost to the manufacturers.   There are
various reasons for this which I will not discuss in the present
paper.   You have been harping on this question of combinations
and trusts for some time.   On one occasion you mentioned a company I am interested in, and held the same up as one of the kinds
of combinations that should be suppressed, and that, too, at a
meeting of an association of laboring men, at a time when you were
a candidate for Attorney-General of the State.   Did you do so then
because you thought it had a bearing on the relations of capital and
labor ?

In these times, when such combinations are a target for all sorts
of newspaper criticisms, as also are our men of wealth, and when
those who are not so fortunate and the young are taught, inferen-
tially, at least, that the rich are despots and enemies of mankind, it
might now and then be well to stop and think a while and consider
the relations between capital and labor ; but not for the purpose of
fomenting the minds of labor against capital.   The question of the
relations between capital and labor has been a theme for discussion
since the first dawn of civilization.   When man first recognized the
rights of his fellow-man, the fatherhood, and the brotherhood, and
the rights of the family, then was the first combination or trust
formed, and civilization had a solid basis for a start.   An ownership
by an unwritten law was acknowledged, which was soon followed by
a division of labor ; and the trades, the arts and the greatest of all
civilizers, commerce.   With these came capital—the result of labor
saved—and by the nature of all things earthly, it is the chief or
ruling spirit of the actions of man.   Why ?   Simply that capital is
the savings of labor; is something to draw from in case of necessity
or sickness.

The average man is a provident being, looking to provide for
his family and self against the accidents of the future.   He is constantly devising ways to accumulate a competency or capital to
draw on in necessity, or to transmit to his family in case of his
death; in which capacity he acts as trustee for those who are to follow him.   A healthy man who would do less, as a rule, is lazy and
not a good citizen.   Capital is a comparative term, and varies as

much in quality or form as in quantity, every man possessing more or less of it. The capital of the teacher is his accumulated knowledge, as is the capital of the lawyer or doctor. After years of study or accumulation they crystallize their capital into a more convertible form, by the use of the same for other people's benefit, for which they receive a compensation in that convertible form of capital called currency, or cash, as you did recently in the canal case, in which you were the leading attorney.   I refer to the case of The State vs. Christy, wherein the combination or trust (partnership) that you represented procured a judgment for the State of $1,500, your fees being $1,660, as shown by the records of the Board of Public Works at Columbus.

The capital of the daily laborer or artisan is his muscle, acquired by practice and training and by a knowledge of weights and measures and the amount of resistance to be overcome, and the best methods to accomplish the results required, intuitively gathered by his daily toil and training, all of which are convertible into cash by a process called commerce, and varying in value in proportion to the skill and ability of the operator, and the supply and demand in the market.   The Great Father, our Creator, did not endow all men alike in muscle or brain or will-power ; hence the unequal chances of men.   Again, all men do not use the talents they have with the same economy, as has been taught us in the parable of the talents in the great Book of Books.   If the definition of the word "capital" —viz, that "it is but labor saved"—be a correct one (and I cannot conceive of a more concise or better definition) then capital and labor are but twin brothers, and should dwell together in peace and harmony in one strong combination or trust.   All things changed from a natural condition for the convenience of mankind, are so changed by labor.   The soil, left to its natural condition, is more apt to produce weeds than grain, hence the necessity for its cultivation.   If all things worth obtaining are but the result of labor, then it follows as a natural conclusion that labor is but a natural condition of civilization, and the better the organization that controls it, the better the results.   Could all men share equally in labor, and were they all equally careful in husbanding and saving the results of labor, then we should have no such contests as now agitate humanity.   Each would naturally fall into some niche in the economy of affairs for which he was qualified.   But such a state of things can only be expected near the end.   Man partakes somewhat of the soil, from which, it is said, he was originally made, and to which we all know he ultimately returns.   If left to himself, without proper cultivation, he becomes a weed and a burden to the soil which he encumbers. Some men are urged on by an inborn ambition to do, because it is natural for them to do; others by pride, some by the love of power and fame, others by necessity. Therefore it does not strike one as being very wonderful that competition is great, and that combinations and trusts are made to overcome it, and that while some minds are abnormally developed others succumb to their less favorable environments and become only human weeds.

Emerson says: " In our society there is a standing antagonism between the conservative and the democratic classes; between those who have made their fortunes, and the young and poor who have their fortunes to make; between the interests of dead labor, that is, the labor of hands long ago still in the grave, which labor is now entombed in money stocks, or in land and buildings owned by idle capitalists, and the interests of living labor which seeks to possess itself of land, and buildings and money stocks. The first class is timid, selfish, illiberal, hating innovations and constantly losing by death. The second class is selfish also, encroaching, bold, self-ruling, always outnumbering the other, and recruiting its numbers every hour by births." He might well have added that the first class, being so very few, and unaccustomed to contend with material things, were slowly being outwitted by the second class, who possess the energy and boldness or the active capital of brain and muscle. The latter class will be found constantly encroaching upon the preserves of the first class by making trusts and combinations, and will, by a natural law of the survival of the fittest in the struggle, build up a new generation of capitalists to take the place of the old, and they will not be the lineal descendants of the old generation, either, but the sons of toil, with their loins all strong with practice and their brains and bodies all healthy and full of energy. Shall these changes, which are constantly taking place and have ever since the "time whereof the memory of man runneth not to the contrary," be peaceful, or shall they be characterized by violence and sore dissensions? is the vital question of capital and labor. Capital and labor are man and wife. And well being and skill are their children. I assume that in our American civilization there are three classes of people : First, the middle class, who outnumber both the other classes; second, the poor, who outnumber the rich; and, third, the rich, who are but few. The latter class recruits, from time to time, its numbers from the middle class ; the middle class, being the one of industry and skill, is ever furnishing active brains and able men to compete for the highest honors, whether the same be for wealth, science, or learning. It is but natural that they make combinations and trusts to achieve their ends. Unfortunately, or fortunately, there is a law of retrogression, as well as a law of progression, to which all classes are amenable. Theref re the poor class is constantly recruiting its numbers from both the rich and middle classes, besides increasing by the natural law of procreation.

Nature has her vigilant police, and, like the police of a well regulated city, she will not permit an idle crowd to assemble on her highways to obstruct progress and commerce, but demands that they move on and up to higher courts of civilization, or else down to the depths of hell on earth. This antagonism is ever present. It is the contest between the right and the wrong, the good and the bad. If you choose the good, nature demands that you pay value received : labor, industry, economy, energy, vigilance, and the gift of continuance in all good. If you choose the bad, your habits will be those of idleness and wastefulness. You will make no trusts or combinations, for you have lost your power of association, and will not work fairly with others. Human laws are but the reflection of the civilization that makes them, and are no more perfect than their makers. Therefore the most of the laws made to regulate capital and labor, or combinations and trusts, have been of little use. The man who cannot see the Creator in the economy of Nature's laws without the assistance of a creed, is but a poor specimen of a thinker. It may be a terrible thought to the transgressor or the weak, yet Nature says that only the fittest shall survive. This rule or law applies as well to capital and labor or combinations and trusts as to anything physical ; the redeeming feature of the law is that all must die, the fittest staying only a little longer.

This law rules in all things human. If a man spends his hard earned money in guzzling beer, his next money will come harder and he will be poorer in strength, and he has also let himself down a degree both morally and mentally. He may join the big crowd that has gone that way before and become a labor crank, and be led on from bad to worse by that other crank commonly known as the demagogue. The latter is a sort of parasite on both capital and labor. He is often a so-called educated man. That is, he has graduated at the high school at public expense, and often has taken higher honors at the expense of his friends, and has become classical. He early imbibes the idea that he is an important personage, before he has learned how to earn his daily bread, and he seeks an even division before he takes any lessons on that subject. He clamors for office; he would rule man before he knows

the first principles of ruling or caring for himself. If he succeeds
in getting an office he becomes conservative until about the time
his term expires; then if his prospects are good for succeeding himself he may be quite decent. If not, he again takes up the cause of
the poor man, and is often mistaken for his friend. He talks and
writes poor men up and rich men down; complains of combinations
and trusts, etc., and is averse to all wisdom that does not agree with
his—the views of a parasite ; rails against labor saved, or capital ;
would abandon all useful machinery, and raises dust generally. If
defeated for office he is a fit candidate for a lunatic asylum, and
he becomes an anarchist and drags as many of his followers
as he can with him. The world is an active one. The people are
progressive. The great masses are the middle classes who believe
in law and order and who are all more or less capitalists or hope to
be, and they will not long tolerate the demagogue or crank. Methods of men are constantly improving. Labor is being saved, and
capital is accumulating. The world has no use for the idle man,
the crank, the demagogue, or parasite.

On the occasion of my first visit to a pine forest in Michigan,
there were impressions made on my mind that I shall never forget.
The day was a perfect one, and a gentle breeze was blowing through
the tasseled leaves of the trees, making music reminding one of the
mythology of the Aeolian Harp. The ground was carpeted with
the fallen leaves of many successive generations, which in turn had
furnished the mold that nourished the tree and kept it ever green
and fragrant. How musical, and yet how still was this closeness to
Nature. One would almost like to make the place a home. However, the thought was only a passing one, and the mind passed on
to visions of lumber in those grand old trunks of trees that reached
far up into the heavens, and that had withstood the winds of many
ages—visions of ships, and houses, of commerce and of trusts, of
capital and of labor; and then you were taken back to Nature as
you noticed that the trees were not all alike. Some were large,
others small. The large ones overshadowed the small and kept
them back and down. And the upper branches of the same tree
overshadowed the lower branches, and the lower branches were
slowly dropping off and the trunk of the tree was reaching up (and
visions of more saw-logs.) Is this all ? No. Nature was coming
to the relief of the little trees. Some of the big trees had sent out
their fibrous roots too far, and capillary action was obstructed and
the big old monarch of the forest was dying. He was getting
punky, and how the little trees began to laugh and grow fat on the

nourishment that the big tree had to surrender. And how the sun's rays that came through the broken and decaying branches of the old big tree made the little one look so gay and bright and happy. How natural it was to compare this forest with a multitude of men. How easy it was to see the little ones and big ones, their aims and ambitions; how grand some looked, and how miserable others. How easy it was to thank God that you were not old and punky. But although not classical, but little, you were ready to grow and had the hope of growing.

Very truly yours,

O. C. BARBER.

No. 2.

Mr. Kohler in Reply to Mr. Barber's No. 2.

HE DENIES THAT TRUSTS HAVE LOWERED PRICES.

SATURDAY, May 25, 1889.

Mr. O. C. Barber.

SIR : I have read and duly considered your letter published in the *Beacon* of last Saturday, and find in it much to approve. In your statement of general propositions and fundamental principles, which occupy so much space, touching the laws of "demand and supply," "capital and labor," "the survival of the strongest," etc., we shall have no occasion for divergence of opinion. I regret, however, that you found it necessary, for want of better argument, to transcend the limits of candid and fair discussion, and indulge in insinuations and innuendoes of a personal nature apparent between the lines : even going far out of your way to bring in the matter of my own and another's account for legal services in behalf of the State of Ohio, in the Canal cases—something in no way connected with or pertinent to the question before us. In such things I have learned to wait with patience and not notice everything that may be said about or against me in the papers or otherwise. If I had space or deemed it necessary, I could easily convince you of the injustice and unfairness of your statement of that transaction.

I shall not imitate your example or follow you in the line of argument sometimes expressed by the phrase, "You are another," but will endeavor to direct what I have to say to the subject. It may have been very much out of place on my part, and I may have

been guilty of great indiscretion in ever opening my mouth on the
subject of our inquiry, or in questioning the expediency and public
policy of a system of combinations in business whereby markets
have been "cornered," fictitious values created, colossal fortunes
amassed, competition circumvented and monopoly the rule in almost every line of industry, not even excepting the necessaries of
life, such as salt and sugar.   The charge of demagogism, which
you bring in such a "railing accusation" will not avail to divert attention from this new order of things, nor will the imputation of
"harping" suppress free speech or intimidate any one.

I have seen something of the evil effects of monopoly and what
these great combinations inevitably lead to.   The matter was
brought to my attention more than once while a member of the
Sixty-sixth General Assembly of this State, and this is why I have
made it the subject of remark on the occasion referred to.   I supposed that you as a "business man," "dealing with material things,"
would have approached the subject more closely; and from your
experimental knowledge of such combinations you would furnish
some facts and figures from actual business, so that the public could
form an opinion as to whether such organizations were in fact beneficial as you claim, or whether, in the language of M. Jevons, an
eminent writer on political economy, "they are conspiracies to rob
the people."   Perhaps you will do so in the future.   We will see.
Mere theories and figures of speech, however fine, are not very instructive.   They prove nothing one way or the other.   The argument borrowed from the Michigan forests, where the tall "pine
trees flourish at the expense of the small trees they overshadow,
until at last nature comes to the rescue, disintegration and decay
set in, and the pine king falls," is very fine indeed; but applied to
human affairs, this law upon which you so confidently rely for the
correction of abuses would take us back to that barbaric age when
the strong man in his strong castle plundered the poor people below
him until a stronger came and despoiled him of his ill-gotten store.
This is harsh doctrine.

Let me examine a few of your statements:

First.   "What I hope to do, is to show that combinations of
capital in the pursuit of any enterprise of whatever kind, when for
legitimate purposes, are perfectly proper, whether such combinations start from a beginning with only cash capital to accomplish
the result, or whether an aggregation of capital invested in any enterprise, but owned by different people or corporations, be consolidated in one combination or trust."

In this complicated statement you are begging the question. What do you mean by *legitimate purposes* ? Do you intend by this, that where a consolidation takes place in any line of business, for manufacturing, by means of a "trust," and the purpose is to limit the production in that line, crush out competition, and fix prices— that that is legitimate ? By your statement below you are assuming the very thing in dispute. I am not discussing an imaginary or ideal trust—such a trust as might be formed if the spirits of just men were made perfect and the Golden Rule was always observed; but I am speaking of trusts as they are in fact, judging of them by their fruits. And as you have not ventured to give us a definition of a trust or tell us what it is, I think it is important in the first place to know just what we are talking about. A trust is a combination of competing concerns, in any line of business, by a pooling of earnings and profits, and by which prices are fixed, and production, if necessary, restricted.

A "trust" is a combination of competing concerns under one management, which thereby reduces the cost, regulates the amount of production and increases the price. It is either a monopoly or an endeavor to establish a monopoly. This is accomplished by presenting to competitors the alternative of joining the "trust" or being crushed out. It is at once a monument of American genius and a symbol of American rapacity.—*Cook on Trusts*, page 4.

The above language is not mine. It is the definition of a learned writer, and describes, in language none too strong, the system of business you have undertaken to defend. The underlying principle of a "trust" and the purpose for which it is formed is to obtain control of the market by crushing out competition; "without that result it is a failure, with it a success." "The modern 'trust' is a monopoly in its purposes, its plans and its culmination." You need not take time to defend associations and combinations for *legitimate* purposes. It is this *"trust"* we are talking about, as it really is, whatever it may plausibly assume or pretend to be. Voluntary associations, corporations for banking, building railroads, manufacturing and trading are "legitimate" and commendable. The laws of every State provide for their organization and management, and the public are protected by reasonable checks and safeguards. But when associations and corporations so chartered consolidate all separate interests so as to give to one board acting for the whole the control of the market, as in the case of the Standard Oil trust, the cotton-seed-oil trust, the sugar trust, the gas trust, and many others I could mention, then the claim of "legitimate purposes" is a pretext, and "monopoly," which common honesty hates, is the fact.

The trust of which I am writing has a mysterious origin and history. It is virtually a secret society. The proceedings of the board of "trustees" are carefully guarded from public view. No newspaper reporter ever gets in to report what has been done. The great sugar trust "covenant" contained the following remarkable provision: "Custody of Deed. This deed, when executed by the parties hereto, shall be delivered to the president of the board, who shall have sole control and independent custody of the same, and the said deed shall *not* be *shown* or delivered to *any* person or persons whatever except by the express directions and order of the board." [The italics are mine.]

If some of these trusts were compelled to make and publish a full report of the organization, the estimated values, watered stock and dividends made, such as banking institutions are compelled to publish each quarter, what a revelation there would be !

If you will not be offended, I will suggest that such a report of the organization, actual condition, assets and net earnings of either of the great trusts with which you are connected, would knock the bottom out of your sentimental theory about the beautiful "pine trees" and the "survival of the biggest."

In the early stages of the trust we find that there was the simple agreement, verbal or written, to fix and maintain prices at a certain point; but, obviously, this form could not last long, because of the advantages gained by some members over the others. Very little objection attaches to such an arrangement. The next stage was an agreement of the same character and for the same object, but it contained stipulations for fines and forfeiture in case of a violation of the agreement. In both these forms of trust the principle of self-interest remained. This was the formative period. To remedy these inherent defects the "close trust was formed, in which all ownerships were removed and the entire property was merged into one company and managed by a single head or board of managers, each member receiving his proportion or share of the profits." (See *Report of Ohio Legislative Committee*, page 5.)

Judged by its results the "close trust" has been the most successful business invention ever devised. Beginning with the Standard Oil trust in 1881, in a single line of trade, it has spread itself over the entire country, until now there is scarcely an article manufactured that it does not control. The result is manifest in the rapid accumulation of enormous wealth in comparatively few hands, instead of being generally diffused, as it ought to be. I have no complaint to make of disproportionate fortunes. They are incident to all civilizations and ages; nor can you destroy human inequalities; but disproportionate fortunes made by unequal laws or monopoly require a change of laws. We are now told that a trust is absolutely necessary to prevent *ruinous* competition; but the committee of the Ohio Legislature, appointed to investigate the subject and report the truth, after looking it all over, visiting different points in the State and hearing all sides, say in their report that they utterly repudiate the claim that competition has become so sharp that trusts and combines are necessary. On the contrary, they reaffirm the old maxim of business, that " 'Competition is the life of trade,' and that any departure therefrom is fraught with danger."—(*Report*, page 4).

In the next place we are informed by promoters and defenders of this scheme that a trust in any business is really of great benefit to the public ; that it furnishes better commodities at lower prices. I deny your proposition that "it is an acknowledged fact that the result of combination has been to reduce the price of articles manufactured," and call for the proof on this point. We are commonly referred to the price of oil, in support of this idea. New oil fields discovered and new processes for refining devised have had more to do with the decline of price than the Standard Oil Co. You affirm that "business is organized for profit;" so it is. It is also organized on a selfish basis, and so long as this is true no combination or "pool," having entire control of the field and the power to regulate the amount of supply and the price to be paid, will furnish an article at cheaper rates than where full, fair and open competition exists.

Much has been said in the past about labor unions, combinations of workingmen to "strike" or stop working, except at a certain price. I submit that strikes have done more harm than good; but no one can complain of such a union of workingmen, if other men who are willing to work at lower rates are left entirely free and unmolested.

In the great Hocking Valley strike other workingmen were brought to the mines who were perfectly willing and wanted to work at the price offered, but they were not permitted to do so. They were intimidated and driven off by violence. Mines were burned and property destroyed and great crimes committed in order to shut out fair competition among workmen and enable the strikers to force the mine owners to accede to the terms demanded.

In the formation of a "trust" the first and most important thing is to get in all competing interests. So long as one remains out there is a "screw loose" in the perfect management of the machine. There must not only be a union, there must be a complete concentration and merging of interests. If any one engaged in the same line elects to stay out and carry on business independently, he must be "frozen out" or crushed. Not long ago I advised a friend of mine to stay out of the combination or trust which was being formed, and keep his property in his own hands and do business as he pleased, and he answered, "They will crush me." The history of the Standard Oil Co. and other companies is full of illustrations of how this can be done most effectually.

    In some lines of business competition is more easily crushed out and gotten rid of than in others. In some trades combination or trust is impossible. Farmers cannot form a "trust." They are still doing business at the old stand and in the old way, except that every article they buy, from barbed wire to salt and sugar, is sold to them at a trust price, and the "wheat trust" fixes the price of the wheat they sell. I see that wheat is quoted to-day at 81 cents. Why is it, with all the new and improved machinery in agricultural pursuits, the reaper, binder, sulky plow, thresher, etc., that the business of farming is so unprofitable and depressed, and the price of land has reached the minimum point? Every few days we hear of a farmer who has made an assignment for the benefit of creditors. Perhaps it is for want of that thorough union and organization which you say is so indispensable in business.

    All that you say in regard to building railroads is true. It requires the capital and enterprise of many persons to do this; but when built and the cars running, we have carefully provided by law that no two or more competing parallel lines of road shall be consolidated. Why is this? Obviously in order that the people, merchants and shippers on the line of these competing roads, may have the benefit of competition. According to your view it is better to let them consolidate and trust for fair and cheap rates to the railway company, as they can do so much cheaper when consolidated. Does not the principle which prevents the consolidation of competing and parallel lines of railroad apply when consolidation of incorporated companies is effected and competition checked or prevented ?

    When we come to the business of banking, we find that in this commercial age such institutions are indispensable, and in nearly every instance they are chartered and the stock owned by many persons who have associated for that purpose.   But banks are organized by special laws, and the public is protected by the most stringent provisions.   The rate of interest is fixed by law.   How would it be regarded if the directors of all the banks in Akron, while maintaining separate organizations, should form a close pool, fix the rates of interest for all and divide the net earnings pro rata ?   If such an arrangement is pernicious and contrary to public policy in the loaning of money, how does it become commendable and proper in the manufacture and sale of salt, sugar and oil?

The fact is, all combinations in restraint of trade, and agreements of that kind to prevent open and fair competition in business, are regarded by the courts as null and void, on the ground that it is contrary to public policy.   It was this plain, well-recognized and just rule of law that Judge Barrett, of the Supreme Court of the State of New York, applied in the recent case brought by the Attorney-General of that State to annul the charter of one of the companies forming the "sugar trust."   The decision of the learned judge in that famous case is a far more complete answer to your argument than anything I can say.   In this case there was a "trust" of about 85 per cent. of the refineries of the United States.   The aggregate capital amounted to $45,000,000.   The object was to control the amount of sugar to be refined and to fix the price of an article of necessary use in every family.   One would suppose that in the manufacture of such an article of prime necessity a solid trust could be formed; but the recent agreement to which I have referred shows how carefully every step was taken.   It was intended to be, and in fact became at once, a monopoly.   As the San Francisco sugar was not in competition, the "trust" at once reduced the output, closed a number of refineries (just as you closed the strawboard factory in the Sixth Ward and elsewhere, in the strawboard trust).   At other refineries the production was cut down and the price of sugar was at once *put up*, so that the increase in price netted the monopoly a profit of $30,000,000 in a year.   Here, then, was a power lodged in a board of managers responsible to no one but themselves, acting under a hidden article of trust, with no check or safeguard to prevent the abuse of power to levy a tax of $30,000,000 upon the consumers of sugar.   I think I need not stop to argue that the power to accomplish such a result by such means is fraught with danger.   All these things came out on the trial of the case of The People against The North River Refining Co., before Judge Barrett, of the Supreme Court of New York, on an application of the Attorney-General to forfeit the charter of one of the companies in the

trust.   The judge held that the agreement or trust was "inherently
unlawful, its tendency being to prevent general competition and to
control prices, and was therefore detrimental to the public and a
legal monopoly." (See *Railway and Corporation Law Journal,*
January 19, 1889, page 56.)   These trust agreements all have a
"goodly outside."   They are very fair and plausible indeed.   The
real purpose is thinly veiled, however, by the phrase "legitimate and
proper purposes."   "A rose by any other name would smell as
sweet."

I do not propose to go largely into detail in this letter.   I will
wait until I hear from one on the *inside;* but I will give one more
sample of business from the wall-paper trust, showing how prices
can be suddenly and arbitrarily raised and lowered to the injury of
the public.   The wall-paper trust was formed six or seven years
ago.   It was an iron-clad affair.   It had a general office in Boston,
and every salesman was obliged to go before a justice of the peace
or notary and make solemn oath not to sell except at the price fixed,
at least not below.   The trust flourished wonderfully until about a
year, ago, when it went to pieces.   The very moment the "pool"
broke, goods that had been selling at $1 sold at 20 cents, so there
was a sudden and unexpected drop of 80 cents.   The result was
that hundreds of small dealers through the country who had bought
a stock at the trust price were nearly ruined by the "drop."   The
fact is that the manufacturers are now engaged, not in fair but in
"cut-throat" competition in order to re-establish the trust on a new
basis.   And this "cut-throat" competition is carried on by means of
the large profits made while the trust was in existence.   Again the
price of a commodity is just as suddenly raised.   The other day I
saw in the newspapers that the "Fruit-Jar Trust" had raised the
price $2 per gross at one jump.

In your search for "precedents" you have happily gone back to
the Confederation of the Colonies, the days of '76.   This is wise and
patriotic.   It is a wonder you did not go still farther back—for instance, to the Garden of Eden.   It would be quite as pertinent to
claim that Adam and Eve got up a "trust" in the vegetable and
fruit trade and failed in the business!   So far as the union of the
Colonies is concerned you ought to know that our ancestors came
in part from England, where the lands are appropriated by feudal
lords and held in perpetual "monopoly" by laws of primogeniture.
Many came from other European countries, where a man's lot in
life was cast by the accident of birth, and where for centuries the
false philosophy prevailed that labor was degrading, and that the

working classes were servile classes.   Liberty and equality of right, contended for on many a disastrous battle-field in the Old World, found at last congenial soil in the American Colonies, and here a government was formed (not a "trust") where equal rights and opportunities might be enjoyed by all.   And if there was one thing that the pioneers of American civilization set their faces against more than another, it was "monopoly and special privilege," or anything that tended in that direction.   Well, in due time after the organization of the Government, laws were passed to levy a tax or duty upon articles imported into this country.   We were in our infancy and had but little capital.   The object, of course, was to *protect* our own industries and give the American manufacturer and workman the American markets.   It was protection against competition from abroad, and was deemed to be necessary to build up our industries.   And from that day to this, whenever it has been urged by those opposed to the policy of protection that such duties constituted a tax upon the people and enhanced prices, and that in consequence a monopoly was created, it has been answered continually and boldly that the claim was false, and that so long as we had full, fair and open competition at home, the price of any protected article would never be higher than the minimum of *fair profit*.   In every political campaign, on the stump and in newspapers, it has been argued and urged in defense of our system of Protection that full and fair competition at home would effectually prevent the exaction of exorbitant and excessive prices.   But now we are told that competition is ruinous!   That full rivalry in business has its drawbacks and must stop, and that to that end the "trust" has been formed and has "come to stay."   So, then, according to this new theory of the trust we must have protection at both ends—protection against foreign competition as well as against competition at home.

Is it advisable that all our home industries, which our laws have for many years protected against foreign competition, should now be handed over to a few very large concerns with great capital and facilities, upon the pretext that competition at home is ruinous?

For many years, indeed ever since the Colonies were united, it has been the policy to encourage competition.   Whatever was in restraint of trade has been looked upon as contrary to the genius of our institutions, and our courts have with one voice declared invalid all agreements having that object in view.   The Supreme Court of our own State 10 years ago, in the case of the Central Ohio Salt Co., used the following language: "Public policy favors com-

petition in trade, to the end that its commodities may be afforded
to the consumer as cheaply as possible, and is opposed to monopolies which tend to advance prices to the injury of the general
public."

Until the advent of the great "oil trust," active, eager, earnest
competition has been the rule in this country, and under its stimulus our resources have been developed and *general prosperity* en-
sued. To change all this and adopt the contrary policy would in
the end inevitably prove disastrous.

One or two things in conclusion : You mention the meeting in
South Akron of workingmen and arraign me for speaking on this
subject there. This is true. I was invited there and while speaking on political issues, my attention was called by an inquiry to the
"strike and riot" in the Hocking Valley, and in that connection I
considered the effects of strikes, combinations and trusts. I supposed
I had a right to do this in a respectful way, and I have no apology
to make for exercising my right to speak or write my sentiments as
I please. .

You said something about lawyers' and physicians' agreements
as to fees and charges. I do not believe in such agreements and
am not connected with any, hence have nothing to defend. About
20 years ago, lawyers had a fee bill here, which never amounted to
anything, and was soon disregarded. Some years ago, when an effort was made to renew it, I refused to sign.

I have given only a few reasons why, in my poor opinion, the
modern "trust," "close trust," or concentrated union, is un-Amer-
ican, unfair and mischievous in its tendencies. I believe that the
old law of business under which we have had so much prosperity, is far better than the modern, exclusive short-cut to great
wealth.

Very truly yours,   J. A. KOHLER.

.   No. 3.

Mr. Barber in Reply to Mr. Kohler's No. 2.

A FORM OF TRUST THAT IS LEGITIMATE.
___

TUESDAY, May 28, 1889.
Mr. J. A. Kohler :

DEAR SIR : In your article published in Saturday's *Beacon*, I
find the following : " In your statement of general propositions

and fundamental principles, which occupy so much space, touching the laws of demand and supply, capital and labor, the survival of the strongest, etc., we shall have no occasion for divergence of opinion." Now, as we seem to agree in a wholesale way, on general principles, I will try and have you agree with me, later on, in a retail way. I quote from your paper again: "I regret, however, that you find it necessary, for the want of *better argument*, to transcend the limits of candid and fair discussion and indulge in insinuations of a personal nature, apparent between the lines," etc. Did you have the same feelings when you mis-quoted one of my sentences and dubbed it with your own parenthesis, "speaking classically?" Or when you were speaking of the argument borrowed from the Michigan forest? Personalities are comparative, like lawyers' fees or trusts and combinations, and will be sized up only for what they are worth. I made no comment whatever as to the justice of your fees, neither do I want you to feel that my word-picture of the demagogue had any application to you. I hold you in too high esteem for that. I only meant the person that I described. You have a perfect right to "free speech" and you cannot get me on the other side of that question, for I intend to be pretty free myself in that line and believe in the principle.

Now to business: You ask me what I mean by "legitimate" purposes. May I answer, that I mean just what the term means according to Webster, nothing more, nothing less, and I have no such hobble-gobble meaning as you suggest.

You seem to think that all schemes of combinations and trusts are but the evil mechanisms of man to swindle the community. Therein you are mistaken. Men of as good repute as you, are engaged in them. Men as honest as you, are engaged in them. Men as just and fair as you, are engaged in them. Men that are as religiously inclined as you, are engaged in them, for the reason that they recognize an economic principle in them, and do not believe they are doing violence to the spinal column of political economy by making them. There may be, and I do not doubt but what there is, a difference in trusts. They are like boys. Some are good and some are *very good;* or like lawyers' fees, some are just and some are *very just.* In my illustrations I will try and be as fair and original as I can, and I will be obliged to you if you will not try, lawyer-like, to lead me into any argument whereby I may be put in the position of defending a wicked boy or a wicked trust, for I do not believe in, or want to take that position. Later in the argument I may try and illustrate how a wicked trust will get pun-

ished and will die; but such a course just now would be premature·
You would overwhelm me with the precedence of dead courts and
the opinions of dead and dying lawyers, while it is the living issues
I must bring out, not in one article, because that would be a wholesale bill, and you know you have acknowledged that you agree with
me on general principles; so let's go into detail in a retail way.
Let us take up one branch of this question at a time, and in doing
so I will put a hypothetical case, viz : A, B and C are engaged in
a business.

No, that won't do ; it will take five more letters than there are
in the alphabet to illustrate the case I have in mind. Therefore, say
that 31 different manufactories owned by as many different people,
companies or corporations, are in a branch of business. The commodity they manufacture being in general use and of large consumption, therefore the public feels concerned for their welfare. I
wonder if I am correct about the last proposition? I guess that I
had better put it that these 31 persons, companies or corporations
are immensely concerned about the public welfare and let you shoot
one proposition at the other and get out of it what you can, using
free speech and permitting no intimidation. These companies
have been competitors in time past ; some have been badly located,
have poor appliances and have had bad managers. Have had frequent failures, but never die, because new capital comes in, but to
make new failures, in which way the life of the trade is kept up.
Under separate management each company must employ from one
to half a dozen salesmen, and for the convenience of customers one
company starts a store in one of the large markets. Thereupon a
competitor does the same, and so it goes until all are represented,
and we have more life of trade. These expenses must be added to
the cost of the goods, making them come higher; but the people must
have the article, and as they encourage the competition they must pay
the price of the cost thereof. In all of these factories there are
elements of strength. Some have one improvement, others another.
Some are located where labor is valuable, or high, others where
labor is not so valuable, or low. It is valuable, so to speak, in one
place, because the expense of living makes it necessary to have a
given amount to make it possible for the operators to live ; and vice
versa. The same rule applies to the commercial part of the business and purchase of material and to the machanical part, machinery, etc.

These are conditions incident to a competitive business. Some
one in your way of thinking, " an enemy to mankind," begins to

analyze the situation. He sizes it up, so to speak. He sees a "job
lot" and goes for it; buys out all these manufacturers, pays them
their price, wrongs no man in the transaction. He says : " I propose to manufacture these goods where they can be made the cheapest. I will combine the talent of the crowd and only use the best
methods and the best mechanical appliances. I will have only three
or four traveling men where the old regime employed 40 or 50. I
will have only one store in New York, where all these different
brands of goods can be had (thus doing no violence to the consumer), instead of half a dozen stores. The same rule applied to
other cities. I will only run 13 factories instead of 31; thus making another saving, making the latter change because in the 13
factories, running up to their capacity, I can make more than the
market demands. Under the old regime several thousand hands
were indifferently employed, many being thrown out of employment months at a time; instead of which I will pick out the best
hands—the ' survival of the fittest'—and give them steady employment; and in this way, by only keeping the best hands, my goods
will be improved. which will give better satisfaction to the consumer, thereby increasing the value of my good will, for those who
are to follow me. In fact, the benefits to myself are accumulative."

Now, this man, company, corporation or trust that has worked
this revolution may be a very good or very bad boy or trust or
what not, giving more or less of the gains made to the public, depending upon his conscience, and how deeply he feels interested in
the public welfare, and how much he values public opinion, and how
much he fears demagogues with their cry of "Down with trusts ! "
If it were my own case, I am free to acknowledge, after taking
proper care of my hands and those interested directly, I would study
very closely the conditions, taking all I could of these savings, keeping in mind only the probability of competition and keeping the
company in order. I would do so, thinking that I could make
proper use of the savings, not expecting to carry them with me into
the next world, but having confidence that I could properly invest
them as trustee for those who are left to follow me. As it is, I sel-
dom have an idle dollar. They are all invested in the enterprises
of the country, employing labor, and in extending the commerce of
the country. And I think I can do you and mankind some good
yet before I shuffle off this mortal coil in the use of the dollars I
may accumulate. Now, Mr. K., I have put to you a hypothetical
case. I have a real one in mind, just like it. Size it up, as it is
put, conscientiously, and show me the wrong that has been done.

Before picking up another item to analyze, please confine yourself
to this one question, digest it, root it to pieces, let us know all about
it.   I fail to know what is wrong about it, if anything.   I ask you
to do this particularly, because you scattered so that I find it absolutely necessary to confine you to one point at a time.

To aid you and to show you the drift of thinking minds, I quote
from a little pamphlet by Erastus Wiman, received this day, entitled "The Waste of Competition."   The author, who is good authority on financial and economic questions, says :

"We are thunderstruck with the expenses from business extravagance, in rentals, clerk hire, or from the cost of living; losses by
bad debts, interest charges, etc.   But all of these expenses and
losses sink into insignificance compared with the losses resulting
from injudicious and hopeless competition.   There are whole groups
of industries; there are great ranges of interests whose profits are
paralyzed by an insane attempt to make money by cutting prices.
The worst part of it, too, is that the public are in no wise benefited.
It costs, for instance, more to keep up two establishments in a small
town than it does one, and yet the business often to be done is   ·
barely sufficient for one.

"Who pays the expense of the second concern ?   Somebody
does, for the children have to be fed and educated; the wife dressed;
the pew rent paid; the house provided for and all other expenses
carried.   Edward Atkinson, of Boston, whose insight into econom-
ical matters is a national advantage, says that it costs more in some
places to deliver bread by the baker after it leaves the oven than it
does to raise the grain, grind the flour, transport it to the point of
consumption, and bake it into loaves.   Now if two bakers' carts are
employed in the delivery of bread, where one would just as speedily perform the task, the cost of the delivery is just double that of
all that it would hitherto cost to produce and handle the grain and
flour.   Who is benefited by the additional baker's cart ?   Certainly not the first baker, for probably all the profits which he had
hoped to make disappear with the advent of the second baker, who
in turn finds that, like the Irishman's goose, 'What is a little too
much for one, is not quite enough for two.'   The only way the two
bakers can continue to exist is to make the public pay the additional expense, which, of course, in the end it does.   So that in this
case, as in ten thousand others, competition does not cheapen, but
becomes an added burden to the cost of existence."

Mr. Wiman, speaking of the Standard Oil Co., says: "Does
any one suppose that petroleum would be as cheap as it is if the

Standard Oil Co. did not exist? This vast monopoly has been most persistently abused; but it has done more to help the world to a cheap and safe artificial light, and thus done more for mankind, · than all the contributions of its detractors combined. The early and wide distribution of American petroleum throughout the civilized universe, the perfect safety of an article which in less careful hands might have been the most dangerous, the infinite variety of uses to which it has been devoted, and above all, its cheapness, are testimonies to the beneficial success of the greatest of combinations in one of the chiefest essentials of existence. In the matter of transportation of petroleum through the facility of pipe lines, conveying by the laws of gravity the raw material from the point of production to the point of manufacture and distribution, a saving has been effected of stupendous proportions for the benefit of the public. Far more has, in this mode of freighting, been achieved by combinations than was ever possible to competition. For the expenditure of $30,000,000 necessary to provide these pipe lines would have been out of the range of possibilities for a score of competitors; the more the competitors the less the likelihood of a beneficial result. In the end, the public pay for all the external expenses incident to competition, one way or another. The obligation must be met. Failure, losses and disasters may come and do come to individuals in the mean time. But in the great balancing up of a series of years, the accounts are squared in the clearing-house of the purse of the public. It must be so, or business would come to a standstill. But meantime is it not a problem that calls for reform, this unlicensed, expensive Saturnalia of competition? "

He closes his remarks with the following paragraph: "It would not be surprising if the writer of these lines should be metaphorically hung, drawn and quartered for presuming to crowd so much heresy into a space so short. But he will have the gratification of knowing that not a few thinking men agree with him in thus giving expression, to what in the minds of a vast number of people must be a latent thought."

Very truly yours,

O. C. BARBER.

No. 3.

Mr. Kohler in Reply to Mr. Barber's No. 3.

MR. KOHLER MAKES SOME QUOTATIONS OF PRICES.

SATURDAY, June 1, 1889.

O. C. Barber, Esq.

DEAR SIR : A word or two by way of preface and I will endeavor to answer your last communication on the subject of trusts.
You say: "Men of as good repute as you, are engaged in them," etc.
Who doubts it ? Certainly I do not; nor have I ever uttered a word
to the contrary, or presumed to make comparisons with any one. I
am entirely willing to accept the word of Mr. Rockefeller, the president of the Standard Oil trust, who, in his testimony before the
committee, speaking of his associates, said : "They are as bright
and able a company of men as ever engaged in an enterprise." The
truth of the above estimate of the men engaged in the business is
shown by the wonderful success of the Standard Oil trust (the pio-
neer company). It was organized in 1882. The trustees have issued
certificates for $90,000,000, of which $20,000,000 was one year's
dividend. The certificates are worth on the market $165, making
the real capital $148,000,000. Its profits some years have been
$20,000,000. These figures are so large that they are really be-
wildering. The case is not overdrawn. (See report of N. Y. Senate
Committee). Twenty years ago the president of this organization
was comparatively a poor man. Now he is (so it is said) the richest
man in the world, and his income is the largest.

In a former letter you define capital as "the result of labor
saved." Whose labor ? Was it Mr. Rockefeller's labor that saved
up this enormous amount of capital ? If so, how he must have
toiled until the drops of perspiration "ran down his face in piteous
chase." Was it other men's labor? or was it the scheme of business we are talking about that enabled the "bright and able men" of
the Standard Oil combination to obtain the lion's share ? You will
probably call this "demagogism," but it is true, every word of it.
It is not individuals or their worth and integrity we are considering.
I grant all you say in that respect. It is the system of business, the
method, or, as you put it, the economic principle that produces such
fabulous results, that alone deserves our attention and interests the
public.

"Coming to business," you specify a form of trust which you
think comes up to Webster's definition of "legitimate," and state

the case with much particularity. I read it over carefully, and so, instead of an actual trust, a real existence, you furnish me the form of a "hypothetical trust" and ask me to digest it, "pick it to pieces," etc. " Hypothetical" means, according to Webster, " supposititious," "imaginary," " a thing assumed without proof," and then you go on and paint the picture of "a good boy" and a " good trust" and say that is the kind of boy.or trust you want to defend, not the " bad boy" or "bad trust." Now, suppose I should turn the tables on you and "hypothetically" give you the case of a " bad boy" or " bad trust," and say, " look on this picture and then on that," we would gain but little in that way.

The country is full of trusts in actual existence. We have them in our midst. I think you said you were connected with one or more. As a business man, you know how they are organized, and for what purpose and what the actual results are. The whole subject has been investigated by legislative committees, and in their reports as well as in the decisions of courts we find what a trust is, and what it accomplishes, and the effect it has upon the public. What good does it do to conjure up cases, good or bad. The real question is, What do the *facts* show ? There is doubtless a difference in trust organizations, as you say, and I am not reflecting upon any with which you are connected; but in my last letter I gave the definition of a trust as ascertained upon actual investigation, where the facts have come out before courts and committees. You have not disputed the correctness of that definition, so we know very well what the system of business is. And I repeat that these great combinations are formed in order to control the market, regulate the amount of product, fix prices and do away with competition. The primary object of a trust is to overcome opposition or competition in business, so that one establishment or concern, on a large scale, can determine what the amount of product shall be and how much shall be paid by buyers. The object of competition is cheapness, or at least it results in that, nothing else. It means more satisfaction to the buyer for less of his labor. Combination is the antithesis of this. It means to get more and give less. Now the question is, which is better for the people at large, combination or competition?

Combination is undoubtedly the thing for the producer, but competition is surely most desirable for the consumer. If we are seeking the "greatest good to the greatest number" we will find that consumers greatly outnumber the producers, and the interests of the former always have and always will be best subserved by open competition. You say there is no combination in the reaper and mower manufacture, yet how could you improve the product ? The price of a reaper is much lower than formerly, and our manufacturers are doing well. In the city of Columbus there are three or more large buggy and carriage factories, employing from 300 to 1,000 men each, all in open competition. They are turning out the best kind of work at a very fair price. You will find that the object of combination is not to benefit the public so much as to benefit the producer. You ask me to take the case you put of the 31 factories and state what objection I have to it. "Size it up," you say. You claim that among the 31, some are badly placed or are unskillful, and among so many concerns there is extra cost and waste. A company or syndicate buys up the "job lot" and all but 12 factories are closed up and only the best workmen are retained. The commodity manufactured is of general use and of large consumption, and your claim is that this (ideal) concern will produce better goods for less money. Possibly this would be so in some far-off "Utopia" or in that golden age of which the poets sing; but my objection to your case is this: The company, in buying up the 31 factories in that line of articles of necessary consumption, becomes master in that line of business. It has absolute control as to the output, price and all that ; and so long as human nature is what it is and business is organized upon a selfish basis you may depend upon it the combination will look out for No. 1. You seem to think that if the trust is a "good boy " it will deal with the public on a fair and equitable basis ; but it depends, after all, as I understand you, upon the conscience of those managing the trust " giving more or less of the gains to the public."

Is it good policy to place such temptations before men ? Is it wise to lodge such power in a single concern ? It might be safe in your hands, but take the world as it is, and men as they are, and the result can be foreseen. What are the actual facts, not "hypothetical cases ? " I have before me the New York Senate's investigation into the "sugar trust." As soon as this combination was formed the price of refined sugar was advanced from three-fourths to one cent a pound. Refined sugar was worth in February, '87, 5.93, but in February, '88, was worth 6.88. More than that difference appears in granulated sugar. How very considerate of the public interests !

In the cotton-seed-oil trust, the business is not confined to cotton seed and oil. It owns lard factories and uses cotton seed to improve hog lard. It at once reduced the price of cotton seed which it used from $7 to $4. The large combination alone enabled it to do this.

In the envelope trust, the amount of product was at once decreased and the price put up. Prices of envelopes advanced from 15 to 20 per cent. by reason of the trust.

In the glass trust the price advanced 10 per cent. by reason of this trust.

The same is true of the " New York meat trust." The price of meat to the consumer was raised while the price of stock to the farmer was lowered.

Brooklyn warehouse trust—Rates on storage of sugar advanced from 10 to 20 cents a hogshead. The trust is to do away with competition. One of the parties, in giving his testimony, said: "We want to destroy *all* we can." " Competition is a bad thing."

The same is true of the gas trust.

Now, I could go on and refer to the milk trust, oil-cloth trust, sand-stone trust, paper-bag trust, steel-beam trust, strawboard trust, and last and most doleful of all, the coffin trust, and in ˙every instance the actual result of the trust was to raise the price. As you are connected in actual business with a number of trusts, would it not be as well to state the facts as to reducing production and advancing prices and earnings, instead of giving *hypothetical* instances.

In my last letter I challenged your statement that it was " an acknowledged fact that combination had reduced prices, especially of refined oil." I called for the proof of this. You have not furnished a single fact, or attempted to do so, but content yourself with a laudatory statement of the Standard Oil trust, from the pen of Prof. Wiman. As you gave no facts or evidence on this point I will do so for you :

From 1861 to 1862 there was no combination. Competition was free during that period. The annual reduction in price was *ten* per cent. From '72 to '81 there was a loose "combine," not very stringent. During that period the average annual reduction was *seven* per cent. From 1882 to 1887 the close trust covered the field and during this period the average annual reduction was only *two* per cent. The actual reduction in the price of refined oil at New York since this trust was organized has been only about half a cent a gallon and the reduction is mainly due beyond doubt to the reduction in the price of crude oil. I give Prof. Andrews as my authority.

I might stop here. But I have one more objection to the process of concentrating or combining the business of the country, on a large scale, in the hands of one or more large corporations or organizations. The evil results of such immense concentration of capital and enterprise are not entirely of a pecuniary character. The question is broader. The time is coming, if it has not already come, when we will not measure everything in this world by the dollar-and-cent standard. "Is not life more than meat, and the body than raiment?"

Time was when a young man, active, eager and energetic, and having a capital of a few hundred dollars, found the door of opportunity open. All the avenues of trade and manufacturing were broad streets, with no barriers across them. Competition was open and free, and a young man could safely embark his small earnings or his inheritance and work his way to the front as a manufacturer and business man. There was little risk. His success depended mainly upon his own efforts.

About 25 years ago you commenced making matches at Middlebury, in this county, on a small capital. Your best capital was your energy and pluck. You had competitors, but your industry, skill and foresight pushed you to the front, and now you are at the head of a large establishment. With all your acknowledged ability as a business man, do you think you could repeat that experiment now? Would you advise a young man, having only $1,000 or more to put up a factory for match manufacture against such powerful odds as now exist? In your own language, would he not have to "buck" against a combination that has its branches in every State of this Union? He might as well try to stand upon the railroad track when the lightning express was approaching. Now this is true in almost any line of business. Young men, unless they have friends or capital sufficient to get into the combinations are prevented from getting into business, or accomplishing what they would accomplish if the field was open. A young man now on reaching the age of 21 with a small capital but plenty of talent and energy will find it very difficult to find an "opening." The field is in truth organized against him and his chances for winning the race are less than they should be.

It is always a serious problem for a young man to get "started in life," as we say. He may have talents, industrious habits, good education and all that. But what to do, what to go at, what trade to take up, or business to learn, are questions rendered more perplexing than even by the fact that business, especially manufacturing, has been so organized, concentrated and combined with large capital as to make it exclusive and an unpromising field of effort for a young man with nothing but his industry and talents.

I had intended, in closing this letter, to ask you a few questions in regard to the organization, working, earnings and profits of certain trusts where you must have accurate and precise information. Such matters have in the past been largely hidden from public view. I supposed you would at your first opportunity furnish a plain business statement of a single industry showing the nature of the organization, capital employed, whether prices were lowered or enhanced, and how much, after the trust was formed, and also the effect of such combination upon the net earnings. I prefer to leave it where you can volunteer the information if you want to.

Yours very respectfully,

J. A. KOHLER.

No. 4.

Mr. Barber in Reply to Mr. Kohler's No. 3.

TRUSTS MUST KEEP IN BOUNDS.

SATURDAY, June 8, 1889.

Mr. J. A. Kohler.

DEAR SIR: In my first letter on combinations and trusts I aimed to show that the modern trust or combination was but a natural condition of commerce or trade; that it was nothing new except in detail, perhaps, but that it was simply a co-partnership, an agreement on a larger scale, incident to the increasing business and magnitude of the trade of this country. In my next letter I endeavored to show the economic advantages of such organizations, which I illustrated, as you stated, by a hypothetical case; but if you had read my article carefully you would have discovered that I stated that I knew of a real case like the hypothetical one and asked you to pick it to pieces.

Well, so far as a multitude of words is concerned, you have said something. But I see nothing as yet that shows that they do not have an economic result, and therefore think that I have so far the best of the argument.

But as I agreed to show how what I style a wicked trust would be punished, I shall endeavor to do so, after which I shall pay some little attention to your letter. Heretofore I have almost ignored them, but as they have some effect on the reading public, I shall give them a little attention. No combination of men can ignore the laws of supply and demand, nor can they formulate any trusts that will be able to do so. The supply of any commodity is always largely governed by the profit that is to be made on the commodity in its production.

SUPPLY AND DEMAND GOVERN CAPITAL.

While there is nothing so cowardly as capital, yet it responds so quickly when the measure of profit will justify, that it seems superabundant, and will come down on you like an avalanche when you have the ability to make it productive; an eager crowd representing the mite of the widow up to the millionaire will claim your consideration. The measure of profit to capital is getting lower and lower. But recently the city bonds of the City of New York, drawing 2½ per cent. interest sold at above par. Under such conditions no well organized or managed combination will demand undue profits, with the view of a permanency of their combination.

In your last letter (No.3) you speak about young men; about their ability to earn money and become prominent in business. You call particular attention to myself in that relation, and ask me if I would like to try the experiment over of rebuilding the concern that I am now at the head of. Let me illustrate : I have been financially interested in the match business as part owner since '61—28 years. Prior to that date I worked in the business for from 50 cents to a dollar a day, and it was good wages, too. Being a strong, hearty boy, having some energy, I felt that I earned the money that I received. Let us see what one dollar a day meant in comparison to the present time. In 1861, parties having money to lend in these parts could easily get 10 per cent. for it. The interest on $3,000 at 10 per cent. represented my entire income for a year's work, $300. To-day we have in our employ young men of no more ability than I had, that we are paying all the way from $700 up to thousands per year. Take the interest at the current rate to-day, six per cent., and a young man getting $900 per year gets the earnings of $15,000 capital. Compare the two. In the first instance, my annual income represented the earnings of $3,000. To-day the annual income of a young man getting $900 per year gets the earnings of $15,000. We have young men in our employ who are getting much more than this. We have older men in our employ who are getting salaries ranging from $5,000 to $7,500 per year; and a dollar to-day will buy infinitely more of the comforts of life than a dollar would 28 years ago.

TALENT COMES HIGH NOW-A-DAYS.

Again, we find it harder work to get the talent we pay the most for, and could find room for men of talent and ability almost any day. Polytechnic schools are educating a vast army of mechanical experts, who, when called upon after some experience, can reproduce, if not improve, almost any mechanical appliance that is now in use. This kind of skill and the cheap capital in the country is a constant menace to high profits in any branch of business ; and notwithstanding what you have said and the terrible illustrations and exaggerations that you have made, about the profits of these combines, there is not one among them who builds wisely and to last, will build on a basis of high profit. It would be an absolute absurdity to try to maintain any monopoly in this country in the manufacture or sale of any commodity without the basis of such monopoly was on low prices and small profits, and they must be further backed up by the ability to produce the goods at the minimum cost and by the most improved appliances. In the case of these syndicates and trusts that have taken undue advantage of the public and have persisted in that course, strange to say, failure has been the penalty.

It therefore does not seem so terrible to me, what is to become of the young men, as it seems to you. Like the little tree of the forest, it must supplant the old dying tree; so will these young men take the places of the older ones in business, and it will not be the drones or the labor crank or the demagogue that will get there, either ; but it will be the one who, by his industry and skill, will have shown himself competent to occupy the position, and he in turn will gather in more idle capital and increase the multitude of workers who will be depending upon him, and they will work along together in the industrial affairs of the country, cheapening their products and bringing peace and good will to all men ; and the greater their success, the greater the consideration that will be shown them, and the less consideration will be shown the errors promulgated by the demagogue.

When I entered into this debate with you, I made up my mind that I would confine myself to general principles and not go into details, as you have frequently urged me to do in your communications. Details that I am not familiar with might be confusing. I did not propose to be accountable for all the mistakes that are being made by trusts and combinations more than you are accountable for all the mistakes that are made by lawyers. We have instances of excesses in all branches of trade and in all professions; but the

mills of the gods, although they grind slowly, grind exceedingly
fine, and the transgressor is usually caught. This question can only
be argued on the broadest grounds. Details in this case are but
incidents in the workings of general principles; but be assured,
wrongs will be corrected, and the mills of the gods will go on grinding. Later in the argument I may specify more particularly, if I
am not already satisfied with what I have said ; but in this paper I
propose to give a little attention to some of the things you have
said, for the purpose of wiping away the cobwebs, so to speak, incident to your looking at the subject through a very small gimlet-
hole, as was suggested to me by a prominent attorney of this
vicinity in commenting on your articles.

A QUOTATION FROM MR. KOHLER.

First I will give attention to a paragraph of your first article,
which reads as follows :

> I have seen something of the evil effects of monopoly and what these great
> combinations inevitably lead to. The matter was brought to my attention more
> than once while a member of the 66th General Assembly of this State, and
> this is why I have made it the subject of remark on the occasion referred to.

I see much of profound wisdom in the above paragraph. Of
course it is not brought out in detail, and about all the information
I can get from it is that you were a member of the Sixty-sixth General Assembly. Let me ask you why you did not give the public
the benefit of your discoveries about monopolies in detail? It
would have been vastly more interesting to the thinking mind than
the declaration that you were a member of the Sixty-sixth G. A.,
and that some one had spoken to you about the subject *more than
once ;* or more instructive than the quotation of the "eminent " M.
Jevons, writer on political economy, who says, " 'They are conspiracies to rob the public.''

By-the-by, I have read much of the current literature on economic subjects and pretend to be somewhat posted, and I have not
yet discovered that M. Jevons was "eminent," and judging from
what you quote, if he has any notoriety, it must be more for the
extravagance of his language than for profound learning. His
language is much in keeping with yours, as noted below:

> A trust is a combination of competing concerns under one management,
> *which thereby reduces the cost* (italics are mine), regulates the amount of pro-
> duction and increases the price. It is either a monopoly or an endeavor to
> establish a monopoly. This is accomplished by presenting to competitors the
> alternative of joining the trust or being crushed out. It is at once a monument

of American genius and a symbol of American rapacity.—*Cook on Trusts,*
page 4.

You followed this by the profound suggestion, "The above
language is not mine, it is the definition of a learned writer, and
describes in language *none too strong*" (italics mine) "the system
of business you have undertaken to defend."

Taking the language of the three, the learned Jevons, Cook
and Kohler, as a guide for extravagance, and assume that you are
all lawyers, I should dislike to have you form a triumvirate in law
and be obliged to submit a case to you. But let us size up Mr.
Cook in detail. He says:

A trust is a combination of competing concerns under one management,
which thereby reduces the cost, regulates the amount of production, etc.

TWO ADVANTAGES OF TRUSTS CLAIMED.

Now, if Mr. Cook had stopped before indulging his extravagance, he would have named two points of vantage in a trust.

First. They reduce the cost.

Second. They prevent waste of over-production.

And if Mr. Cook had finished his paragraph as follows it would
have been more in keeping with the facts, viz: The enormous savings incident to this mode of doing business by reducing the cost of
production and preventing the waste of overproduction, have made
the modern trusts so profitable that they seem like very monopolies.
Small concerns with poorer appliances and less capital, being unable
to compete, prefer to sell out rather than to be crushed out by the
superior methods of the larger concern. This, in my way of
thinking, would have made his conclusions more profound, and he
would not have led his brother Kohler, whom he inspired with such
terrible thoughts, to give such poor advice to a friend, viz: To not
go into a trust.

There are some things about the trust that, looking at it as you
do, through a gimlet-hole, you cannot see clearly. Let us illustrate:
There is only a given amount of any one article consumed and
only a given number of people can be profitably employed in producing the article. Now, for profit, it is of the utmost importance
for cheap production that the methods employed be the best, and
then what is gained by said methods is so much gained to the
public. It is so much labor saved, or so much capital accumulated.
It makes but little difference who temporarily holds these gains;
sooner or later the public gets the benefit, either directly or indirect-
ly. As instance the donation of Rockefeller of $600,000 for edu_

cational purposes, which seems to be a little surplus that he can take
from his immense accumulation for outside purposes.   I dare say
all the other gains that he has are actively employed in the industry
he represents, and you know you have acknowledged in one of your
letters that difference in wealth is no crime.   This, all clear in
your mind, you will certainly not abandon what is good about the
modern trust; especially, Mr. Kohler, as you are of a compromis-
ing mind, as is shown by the following *sop* thrown out to the work-
ingman in one of your letters :

> Much has been said in the past about labor unions, combinations of
> workingmen to strike, or stop working, except at certain prices.   I submit that
> strikes have done more harm than good ; but *no one can complain of such a union
> of workingmen, if other men, who are willing to work at lower rates are left entirely
> free and unmolested.*

How the words in your profound conclusion jingle. "What
boots it, gentlemen of the jury" if workingmen do form a union,
if they do not strike and prevent others from working ? "What
boots it, gentlemen of the jury," if people in one line of trade
make a trust, so long as they do not prevent others from doing the
same thing ?

I quote again from your paper as follows : "All that you say in
regard to building railways is true.   It requires the capital and enterprise of many persons to do this.   But when built and the cars
running, we have provided by law that no two or more competing
parallel lines of road shall be consolidated. Why is this ? Obviously, in order that the people, merchants and shippers on the line of
these roads, may have the benefit of competition.   According to
your view, it is better to let them consolidate and trust for fair and
cheap rates to the railway company, as they can do so much cheaper
when consolidated.   Does not the principle which prevents the consolidation of competing and parallel lines of railroad apply when
consolidation of incorporated companies is effected, and competition checked or prevented ?"

I am opposed to the principle that prevents consolidation. I
believe in the rights of property, and do not want such men as you
to say whom it is proper for me to consolidate my property with.
To my mind it is very absurd for a man who, if he employs another,
the range of employment only reaching from blacking your boots to
driving your team, to say to others what they shall or shall not do.

ANTI-CONSOLIDATION LAWS OF NO EFFECT.

Again, the laws preventing consolidation of parallel lines of
railroad are all just so much waste paper, so far as the effects on the

management are concerned; and I will cite you one or two cases as evidence : The Hudson River Railroad, New York Central Railroad, Lake Shore & Michigan Southern, form one continuous line of railway from New York to Chicago. And although they are separate organizations, they are practically under the same management, and are paying properties. The stock being widely distributed and owned as investments by thousands, widows and orphans having their share, yet the controlling interest is in the hands of but few. It occurred one day to a few capitalists that this line was making more money than the capital invested warranted. Thereupon they constructed the West Shore road, running from New York to Buffalo, and Nickel Plate road running from Buffalo to Chicago, paralleling the first system. By so doing the public found the life of trade in the competition engendered. Widows and orphans, the aged and decrepit, who had accumulated a competency and invested it in the first line, were cut off from their income, and you had a competition that prostrated the trade of the whole country, and which, if it had been kept up, would have bankrupted every east and west railway in the country, and no doubt effected other ills, and in fact was liable to throw the whole country into a panic.

At this juncture, the Vanderbilt crowd came to the rescue, and bought out the West Shore and Nickel Plate roads, and now these two parallel roads are under the management of the same people. Can you explain to me, Mr. Kohler, by what methods óf reasoning you arrived at the conclusion that it is better for the country that these roads, being owned by one party, should be kept under two separate organizations when there is economy in organizing them under one ? The result in rates to the public can not be lessened by having two organizations to keep up where one would do as well. In the mean time, the mills of the gods are still grinding.

Until the government took the matter up and passed the Inter-State Commerce bill, railroad rates were constantly being reduced; but since, they are going up. Such is the result of legislation.

THE FARMER AND THE TRUSTS.

I quote again from your first letter:

In some lines of business, competition is more easily crushed out and gotten rid of than in others. In some trades, combination or trust is impossible. Farmers cannot form a "trust." They are still doing business at the old stand, and in the old way, except that every article they buy, from barbed wire to salt and sugar, is sold to them at a trust price, and the " wheat trust" fixes the

price of wheat they sell.   I see that wheat is quoted to-day at 81 cents.   Why
is it, with all the new and improved machinery in agricultural pursuits, the
reaper, binder, sulky plow, thresher, etc., that the business of farming is so un-
profitable and depressed, and that the price of land has reached the minimum
point?   Every few days we hear of a farmer who has made an assignment for
the benefit of his creditors.   Perhaps it is for want of that thorough union and
organization which you say are so indispensable in business.

Do you mean to imply that these results are produced by trusts?
If so, why don't you specify and state wherein the result is produced?
Or is this but an artful dodge, appealing to the farmer for his influence on your side of the question?   Is wheat any lower to-day than
it was 30 years ago, and is not the labor of producing wheat much
less than it was 30 years ago?   Ought you not to look for the correct solution of this question for the farmers?   Is it not a fact that
the cause of the reduction of farm lands in this section is owing to
the vast extent of agricultural districts being opened up where land
is $1.25 an acre instead of $60 per acre? and the competition thus
engendered producing the results that are so dreadful and lament-
able, as stated by you?   Certainly these results are not produced
because the price of coal oil is too high, for it has never been so
low in the history of its production as to-day, as in all the articles
you name.   I can see how the taxes of the farmer may have been
increased by the fees of lawyers, as in your own case.   I am told
you and your associates brought a bill for services in the canal
cases, once referred to, of over $2,800, and the result thus far is only
a judgment of $1,500 in favor of the State.   Who had to pay these
expenses?   Why, the land owners, and those who pay taxes.   You
may call this personal, but is it not applicable?

I might go on and riddle your letters from beginning to end and
show false conclusions and misstatements, but that would make it
more of a personal contest and we would get further away from the
question at issue ; but I think I have given you enough to digest
for one meal.   The world is full of evil.   It may be found in trusts
as in the common avocations of life.   But I have the utmost faith
that it is getting better, and that the conditions of mankind are constantly improving.   And I am not convinced yet, nor can I be by
the job-lot arguments of every labor crank and demagogue, or by
any argument that you have thus far produced, that trusts are the
all-important thing to be legislated on.   You speak of an investigating committee by the Ohio General Assembly on this subject.
You hinted at wonderful discoveries, but, as usual, did not specify.
Under the circumstances it is perfectly proper that I refer to the

conclusions of a similar committee appointed by the General Assembly of the State of New York. I quote from their conclusions as follows:

NEW YORK ASSEMBLY COMMITTEE ON TRUSTS.

"Competition vs. Combination.—Whoever has studied this question must have learned that competition, which is called the 'life of trade,' is not without its evils, and that combination, which is commonly considered its antithesis, is not without its advantages. The aid of law for the prevention of trusts is usually invoked to protect the weak individual against the strong combination, and yet every day, in the world of commerce the weak individual is overcome by his strong competitor, who has more money, more credit and other greater advantages than he. In the world of nature everywhere this rule prevails—the weak are overcome by the strong" [like the big tree overshadowing the little tree], "and nothing lives or thrives but at the expense of something else which was in some measure its competitor. The effects of excessive competition are nowhere better illustrated than in the history of those competitive wars with which the public are already too familiar, in which great railway, telegraph and manufacturing corporations sacrificed fabulous wealth, the property of innocent stockholders, in the endeavor to secure the occupation of some particular field of enterprise, to the exclusion of every adversary. Such contests often result in wounds which it takes long years to heal, and from them the public not only receives no real benefit but positive injury rather ; for sooner or later the public is expected to make good the losses which such ruinous policies entail. Wars of this sort between individuals often result in disaster for one or both contestants, but when carried on by great corporations representing vast properties held by them as trustees for stockholders, the ruin or injury of one or all contestants becomes a national calamity.

THE TRUST NOT INDIGENOUS.

Again : " It should, however, be borne in mind that the trust is not indigenous to this age or country only ; that in one form or another it has existed in every prosperous commercial community from the most remote and primitive ages in every part of the world, and among every people of whose social institutions we have any information. It would seem reasonable to conclue that phenomena of such wide development in the world of trade must be the result of natural law, which, while it might be advantageous to the people to be subject to reasonable artificial restraint, still exists, like all natural law, for some useful purpose ; and that its total destruction, even if such a result could be brought about by laws of our own making—a fact which is extremely doubtful—instead of contributing to the public welfare, would be the greatest of public calamities."

Again : "Combination rarely exists except as the result of excessive competition. In the natural condition of affairs the law of supply and demand primarily fixes the reasonable and natural price of every commodity. But under the stimulus of excessive competition, when each competitor seeks to drive his adversary from the field of trade or transportation, new elements, good and bad, enter the problem, and each rival—not for the public good, but for his own advantage—with rapacious ingenuity, lessens the cost to the consumer below the natural and reasonable price ; and that he may do this without sacrifice to his capital he increases the product, cheapens the expense of manufacture by cheaper methods and processes, and all with the expectation of ultimately controlling the market and ruining his adversary. But the cheapness of the price is temporary only, for each producer, manufacturer and common carrier expects, when his competitor is driven off or destroyed, to be able to fix the price, and for a while, at least, to oblige the public to pay a sum in excess of that which, in its normal operations, would be required by the law of supply and demand. Combination to increase the price is often the way of escape sought from this state of affairs. That combination is the natural result of excessive competition there can be no doubt. The history of the copper trust or syndicate" [which came to grief by its excessive naughtiness], "the sugar trust, the Standard Oil trust, the American cotton-seed-oil trust, the combination of railroads to fix the rates of freight and passenger transportation, all prove beyond question or dispute that combination grows out of and is a natural development of competition, and that in many cases it is the only means left to the competitors to escape absolute ruin.

OLD LAWS REGULATING COMBINATION.

"The activities consequent upon successive competition, always most numerous in thrifty and progressive communities, and which lead sometimes to monopoly, and naturally to combination in one form or another, have always been subjects of legislative and judicial disapproval and restraint. At common law, many of these forms of business were declared to be misdemeanors. Contracts in restraint of trade were held to be void, as contrary to public policy. Forestalling, regrating and engrossing, the effects of which are claimed to be similar to those of combinations and trusts, were punishable by fine and imprisonment.

" Forestalling the market was declared by statute to be the ' buying or contracting for any merchandise or victual coming in the way to market, or dissuading persons from bringing their goods or provisions there, or persuading them to enhance the price when there, which practices make the market dearer to the fair trader.

" Regrating is described by the same statute to be ' the buying of corn or other dead victual in any market and selling it again in the same market or within four miles thereof.' "

What an absurdity such a law would be in this age ! After quoting similar laws equally absurd, they say : "Unreasonable as these provisions were, prosecutions under them met with popular approval, and funds were raised by the public to continue the prosecutions. These offenses were abolished in England in 1844. It is claimed, with some degree of assurance, that they are still misdemeanors in this State. Whether they are or are not offenses still punishable by the criminal law here, it will hardly be disputed that society has outgrown these antiquated and unreasonable provisions, which only aggravated the evils which they were intended to abate. They had their origin in a state of affairs when governmental interference in the details of social and commercial life existed to a degree which in this age would be intolerable. They were contemporary with and of the same spirit as laws fixing the price of certain clothing, and punishing by fine and imprisonment whoever should sell it at a price above that fixed by law; and that no servant in husbandry or common laborer or servant to any artificer should use or wear any clothing or cloth above a certain price."

Mr. Kohler, would you like to go back and reinstate some of these laws in our land?

They further say on class legislation: "This was class legislation indeed, and its promoters seemed to have thought that economy in living, suitableness of apparel and general prosperity in public and private affairs, could all be accomplished by acts of Parliament. The history of all endeavors to impose unreasonable restrictions upon the trade, the customs or even indulgences of a people *prove how vain all such efforts are.*

"The history of the law relating to contracts in restraint of trade, which it is claimed have the same tendency as combinations or trusts, is interesting, as illustrative of the growth of an enlightened public opinion and the facility with which the courts, the most conservative branch of every government, respond to it.

BUSINESS TRANSACTIONS UNTRAMMELED.

"The first reported authority relative to contracts of this character is found in 1415, in which the court held that a bond in which the defendant bound himself to refrain from carrying on a certain employment for six months in the city of London was void, as being in restraint of trade. The courts, after many years, modified this rule, and held that a man might agree to refrain for a certain time to pursue his calling in a particular place without injury to the public, and that such a contract could be enforced at law upon the theory that contracts in partial restraint of trade were not necessarily contrary to public policy. Later still, the courts expanded the rule so that contracts limited in time and to a particular territory not embraced in the Kingdom were not obnoxious to the rule. A decision has recently been made by the court of last resort in this State (The Diamond Match Co. *vs.* Roeber, 106 N. Y., 473) settling the law of New York upon this subject. The opinion in that case states: 'It is clear that public policy and the interests of society favor the utmost freedom of contract within the law, and require that business transactions should not be trammeled by necessary restrictions.' And the opinion of an English court is quoted with approval: 'If there is one thing more than another that public policy requires, it is that men of full age and competent understanding shall have the utmost liberty of contracting, and that contracts, when entered into freely and voluntarily, shall be held good and shall be enforced by the court of justice.'

"The Court held that the covenant that defendant would not for 99 years engage in the manufacture of a certain commodity within the United States or Territories, except in the State of Nevada and Territory of Montana, was good ; and the opinion stated further that 'a party may legally purchase the trade and business of another for the very purpose of preventing competition, and the validity of the contract, if supported by a consideration, depends upon its reasonableness as between the parties.' In the application of the rule, there has been gradual enlargement until it has become merely nominal in this country as between individuals at least. In Leslie *vs.* Lorillard (110 New York, 519), which proved the validity of a contract between certain steamboat companies (corporations) to restrain competition, the compact was held good. The Court in that case used the following language, which comes very close to the subject of this inquiry : 'At the present day there is not that danger (from contracts in restraint of trade or competition), or at least it does not exist to an appreciable extent, except, possibly, as suggested in the case of corporations. In their supervision and in their restriction, within the limits of their chartered powers, the Government and the public are directly interested. Corporations are great engines for the promotion of the public convenience and for the development of public wealth, and so long as they are conducted for the purposes for which they were organized they are a public benefit, but if allowed to engage without supervision in subjects of enterprise foreign to their charters, or if permitted unrestrainedly to control and monopolize the avenues of that industry in which they are engaged, they become a public menace, against which public policy and statutes design protection. * * *   I do not think that competition is invariably a public benefaction, for it may be carried to such a degree as to become a general evil."

This New York report further stated, under the heading, "The Necessaries of Life :" " Of all combinations, those which manufacture and deal in what are called the necessaries of life are least to be feared, for the sources of such products are world-wide, are in a state of constant activity, and cannot be controlled or even effected for any length of time by capital, however large. The history of the copper syndicate (*Societe des Meteaux*), as given in the testimony taken by the committee in the City of New York in November last, aptly illustrates the utter inability of any combination for any length of time to limit the product or unduly fix the price of any of the world's great commodities."

The Committee concludes as follows : "In conclusion, your Committee would frankly state, while the trust, which is a new form of an old and well-known principle, is full of dangers and should be hedged around by law, it is not of necessity a monopoly nor inconsistent with the public advantage within certain reasonable limitations ; that every combination in trade has greater power either for good or evil than the individual members of which it is composed ; that its power to fix prices or unduly increase them is indeed greater, but that the danger arising from its exercise is greatly lessened by the inventions and discoveries of this age ; that steam and electricity are factors of the greatest consequence in the adjustment of wrongs and differences, which in former times would have been without remedy ; that the new elements on which the principle of combination seizes are balanced and offset by other and, if possible, more powerful forces of modern civilization ; and that, as a general rule, society may rely upon these opposing elements and compensations to keep the peace between it and the conflicting interests and influences of the world of trade, no matter how great their interests and influences may be, and that such balancing forces *are far more patent to that end than any arbitrary rules or legislative enactment.* Combination among laborers or the right to unite for protection is a principle still recognized by law. The limits within which such right may be exercised are plainly designated, and sharp penalties are prescribed for those who overstep them. The principles upon which such rights were formerly denied bear a remarkabls resemblance to those which are now urged to deny absolutely the right of combination to capital.

"The right of combination among capitalists, manufacturers, or common-carriers for every purpose consistent with the public welfare should not be unnecessarily restrained ; but the severest penalty should be prescribed and enforced (and unless enforced it should not be prescribed) for every attempt at combination, the end and purpose of which is an unjust monopoly or of unduly lessening the price of any commodity.

"This investigation, ordered by the Senate, has not yet resulted in any legislation on this subject. But the investigation has not been without great public advantages. The more that is known of trusts, the less they are feared. There has been a remarkable change in public opinion regarding them since the commencement of the investigation. It is a growing sentiment that the evils of which they are the cause are short-lived. The result justifies the deliberate course of the Legislature regarding this question."

Now, Mr. Kohler, I think in my several articles that I have proved what I hoped and started out to do—viz, that combinations of capital for the pursuit of any enterprise of whatever kind, when for legitimate purposes, are perfectly proper, whether such combinations start from a beginning with only a cash capital to accomplish their result, or whether an aggregation of capital, invested in an enterprise, but owned by different people or corporations, be merged in one combination or trust. I have been sustained in the legitimacy of such combinations by the investigation of the Committee on Trusts appointed by the New York General Assembly, and by the decisions of the courts relating thereto. Please remember that I am not defending any of your will-o'-the-wisp bugaboos, nor do I belong to any trust or combination that has any other purposes than legitimate purposes in view.

Very truly yours,

O. C. BARBER.

———————

No. 4.

Mr. Kohler in reply to Mr. Barber's No. 4.

PROFITS AND PRICES—HOW TRUSTS AFFECT THEM.

———

Saturday, June 15, 1889.

O. C. Barber, Esq.

DEAR SIR : Your letter of five columns in Saturday's *Beacon* has been duly considered. Aside from the report of the New York committee on trusts (which you copy entire) I find nothing new and nothing to answer except the glittering generalities and jumble of platitudes with which you begin and end every letter. These have become threadbare from constant use and should be put aside. What your case really needs, and what an interested public had a right to expect at your hands, is a plain statement of facts of a business nature, such as a practical man standing on the ground floor of an actual trust is not unfamiliar with, but knows all about, and could explain every detail of the organization, purposes, stocks, valuations, trust certificates, and ways and means of the business we are talking about.

MORE DETAILS WANTED.

You have had an excellent opportunity to put your practical knowledge of such affairs to good account. The key of the combination is in your hands ; you can open the door of secrecy and disclose what a trust combination is, in the full tide of successful operation ; whether it enlarges or curtails production, and whether prices are increased or lessened and the reason for it ; how it affects workingmen, in giving more or less employment ; the result to the consumer and the profit to the producer. I *have* urged you to bring out these matters because we are considering things as they are in fact, and not merely in profession ; an *actual* condition and not a mythical existence. But on all these practical questions you have not a word of explanation, but are as silent as the Sphinx on the banks of the Nile, and your excuse is the following : "When I started in this debate I made up my mind that I would confine myself to general principles and not go into detail, as you have frequently urged me to do in your communication; *details that I am unfamiliar with might be confusing."* (Italics mine).

Exactly ! How about *details* (such as any one knows) you are familiar with. Even now, while I am writing, you are engaged in consolidating and arranging the new American strawboard trust just transferred to, and incorporated under, the laws of Illinois and modeled after the whisky trust, to continue and perpetuate the monopoly of the "Union trust." And yet you are not familiar with details ! Fiddlesticks ! Instead of logical reasoning, from actual facts, real business, tangible things, you are soaring among the "mills of the gods," and shouting yourself hoarse over the demagogue, communist and crank. You play upon these names, not as on a "harp of a thousand strings," but as on an old fiddle with one string. And as you draw the bow back and forth, it is the same old tune—demagogue, communist and crank.

If to question the nature and methods of trust combinations, by which the few engaged in them become quickly and immensely rich at the expense of the public ; if to deny the right of a board of trustees, representing a consolidation of corporate interests, to arbitrarily " corner " the market in any line of production, curtail the supply and force prices up as self-interest and avarice may require, constitute a demagogue, then you will find the land full of them, for the people, who can only know the tree by its fruits and judge the cause by its effect, have found that there is something unequal, oppressive and wrong in the principle of these vast consolidations that have been and are bringing about great " deals " in railroads and other business interests and property, and in which gigantic speculations and unjust exactions go hand in hand.

A REMEDY WILL COME.

Such being the case a remedy will come in due season, not through the demagogue or crank, but by the people. Both the great political parties in this country, in their conventions, have passed resolutions condemning trusts and thereby pledged themselves to oppose them by proper laws. In the United States Senate, Senator Sherman uttered his indignant protest against them, and introduced a bill (now pending) to prohibit or regulate the matter. In the State of Missouri a law has just gone into effect to prohibit "trusts," and "pools." The Supreme Court of our own State a few

years ago, in the case of the salt trust, declared against all such
combinations in the strongest language, while the decision of Judge
Barrett, of the New York Supreme Court, annulling the sugar combination, by taking away the charter of one of the corporations,
show how such transactions are regarded in courts of justice, and
whether they are legitimate or not.

The report of the committee which takes up so much space in
your letter, is an authority against you. "The trust is full of dangers," it says, "and should be repressed and hedged around by
law." It says more should be done where monopoly is attempted.
In the light of so many concurring opinions and from such sources,
"hard words break no bones," and you are only sawing the air in
impotent denunciation.

CAUSES OF COMMUNISM AND STRIKES.

In this connection a few words about "communists" and
"strikes." Has it not occurred to you that the rapid accumulation,
not of riches merely, but of immense fortunes and the concentration
of millions of money in comparatively few hands, through the in-
strumentality of syndicates, pools and trusts, all over this land ; the
injustice and wrong that often attends such accumulation and not
unfrequently the cutting down of wages and sudden discharge from
employment, has done more to excite a feeling of discontent, to encourage gambling speculations in stocks and "deals" and a disre-
gard of law than all other causes combined ? The fact is proved
that many of the great combinations with vast capital at command,
as well as the business talent which you say comes so high, have
sent their agents to nearly every country in Europe to bring workingmen here by the ship load in order to obtain cheaper labor than
could be obtained at home. And in the great cities like New York,
St. Louis and Chicago, in every riot, strike and communistic demonstration, this ignorant element has been conspicuous. It is in
these places the red flag is waved.

I copy the following from the report of the Ohio Bureau of
Labor Statistics just issued (12th report):

> The labor riots that now and then occur are almost without exception the
> work of men who were brought up by the agents of these trusts and imported
> into this country to take the place at reduced wages of American workmen.

I am merely noticing as I pass along some of your remarks. I
will not dwell upon your second reference to the fees of myself or
associates in the canal cases. Suppose I should, for the sake of the
argument, concede all you say and insinuate in that respect. What

of it here? Does it make our hair white or black, so far as trusts
are concerned? I think when you reflect that I came into this
debate wholly upon your request, that it will gradually dawn upon
you that you are only weakening your case, and exhibiting your
discomfiture. We are discussing trusts now. And it is better to
attend to one thing at a time. Wnen this is concluded the door
will be open to investigate the other matter, if you wish. I refuse
to be diverted from the main question.

One thing more : In your opening paragraph you assert that you
think you "have the best of the argument." I will not dispute with
you on that piont. I am willing that you should think so, and possibly with the exception of the "prominent attorney" (whose name
you need not give) no one else may say so. It is proper, of course,
that a man should be judge in his own case, and equally in good
taste, to decide the case in his own favor. I do not know whether
I have the best of the argument or not. My greatest concern is to
get the facts before the people. It is no new experience for me to
be beaten in argument. I am cheered, however, with the reflection
that I did not go about it with a "chip on my shoulder" issuing
challenges like Philistia's proud chief, and that I am here with only
a simple sling, such as shepherds use ; and a few smooth stones
which I gathered from the brook.

POINTS OF DIFFERENCE.

We have been discussing the question from widely different
standpoints. I have endeavored to show what a real trust is ; the
purposes of the consolidation, and what, in fact, it does, as shown
by the results. You have presented an ideal trust, such as it may
be under certain conditions, limitations and qualifications. It is
only the good and legitimate trust that you can see ; but as you
do not name one, or indicate what its business is, we are left in the
dark as to what you mean by legitimate purposes. Show me one such
an organization and I will name ten that have had no other object
than to obtain control of the market, and having obtained that, by
buying up competitors or killing them off, have curtailed the product in order to increase the price. Such a trust is a bad trust on
the ground of public policy. And when articles of necessary use
are the subjects of such combinations, the public who use them are
placed at the disadvantage of having a tax put upon them whenever
it suits the interest of a board of trustees to do so.

NATURAL LAWS WRESTED.

Under natural laws, such as demand and supply, the product

will always be regulated by the demand and the cost regulates the price. Combination raises prices. Competition cheapens the price. When the latter exists the lowest possible cost, plus normal profit, should measure the price. A trust combination means force, setting all natural regulations at defiance. It is an artificial contrivance to hold the product in check, regardless of demand, so as to create more or less of a scarcity and by that means raise the price. Under such conditions the trust possesses the power to fix its buying and selling prices by an arbitrary standard.

It can buy what it requires to manufacture at the lowest cost and sell what it produces at the highest price. In the cotton-seed-oil trust, for instance, large quantities of cotton seed are used (700,000 tons were crushed last year). Before the trust came into power it was selling at $7, but at once this was reduced to $4. The meat combination in New York reduced the price to the farmer from whom stock was purchased and raised the price to the consumer. So with the milk trust and others I might name.

STATEMENTS THAT WERE IGNORED.

In my last letter I gave you the names of more than a score in number of the leading trusts and furnished you items taken from official investigation and from the reluctant testimony of the parties themselves, showing that in each and every instance, as soon as the consolidation was effected and competition substantially at an end, a reduction of product and advance of price followed. You took an entire week and wrote up five columns in answer, and yet you failed to point out a single error in the statement, and gave it no attention, "ignoring" it, as you say. Now the whole question is: Is it good policy to do this? Does it benefit or injure the public? Professor Andrews, of Cornell University, says in such case, if the article is a necessity, "they may bleed the public to death."

I note the closing statement of your letter :

> Please remember that I am not defending any of your will-o'-the-wisp "bugaboos," nor do I belong to any such trust or combination that has any other purpose than legitimate purposes in view.

HOW THE STRAWBOARD TRUST WORKS.

In this connection, I may refer to what is a matter of current history in regard to the strawboard business. Such reports are not always true, and if there is any error in this statement I would be glad to be corrected. I only want to show that in this, as in every enterprise, self-interest prevails, as it always has and always will prevail, so long as men are human, whether he be a lawyer, doctor or manufacturer.

Prior to July, '87, the making of strawboard was carried on by a number of independent concerns through the country, in competition. Strawboard was selling, as I am informed, at $37.50 per ton. At the above date a consolidation of all these separate concerns was effected; a trust was formed. Not all of the plants were in. There was a large factory in the Sixth Ward, this city, employing perhaps 100 men. It was a strong competition. There were four or five others, at other points. All of these were bought up at an aggregate cost of half a million dollars. The one in the Sixth Ward must have been making money rapidly at $37.50 a ton. It must have been a very valuable property indeed, for you paid. $175.000 for it. As soon as these purchases were made and the factories at these places were closed, the workmen in them were unexpectedly and suddenly thrown out of employment. You will not claim but whnt the object was to produce less strawboard. With this in view, the number of workmen must be reduced. This, of course, affected the price. A small supply increases the price; and the next thing done was to raise the price of strawboard $5 per ton. But this did not stop here. In a short time another $5 per ton was added, so that $10 per ton was the added cost to the consumer. Under natural conditions prices as a rule go up or down gradually, and do not jump in this way. Nor are large manufacturing establishments closed up by wholesale in that way except in cases of insolvency.

In the February following, one of the concerns in the trust, and the only one in the county in operation, declared a dividend of 37½ per cent. If this represented the earnings for one year, with the tax of about 2½ per cent. added it would only take about two and a half years to double the investment. Such results, it seems to me, are only possible where there is substantially no competition. Now, I think that the system of business, called a trust, that enables all or a majority of concerns in any line of production to virtually place a tax upon consumers in that way is wrong in principle and unfair in operation. The fault I find is in the system of business. I am not judging any one in this matter.

The truth is, Mr. Barber, corporate power has its uses and abuses, and this is even more true when integration of corporations takes place. Individual responsibility is lost. Corporations are things, machines, aggregations, and, as Lord Coke says, they are

4

"soulless," and as every one knows, many things take place in the way of "deals," "operations" and "speculations" that men would not do where individual responsibility stood at the front. The zeal for money-getting in this country has become a consuming passion. The multitudes are rushing by. The example of great fortunes suddenly made, and the power of money, has stimulated not only business enterprises but all manner of speculative devices, "corners," and contrivances to make it at once. But this belongs to ethics, so I will drop it.

WHAT THE LAW SHOULD REGULATE.

It is the province of law to regulate our affairs as may be just and equitable. Hence we have usury laws, and the rate of interest is fixed at a price. This is done in order to protect the needy borrower. If men, as a rule, were exactly just and could be relied upon in all cases, such laws would not be necessary. Again we have laws regulating the rate of charge for railroad travel. Now, if railroads were all good, or "good trusts," and power and opportunity were never turned to selfish account, such laws would not be necessary. Nevertheless our law fixes the rate at not exceeding three cents per mile, and now we have the Inter-State Commerce law designed to prevent the shameless discriminations practiced by the great railway combinations, in the interest of fair competition. The investigation last year brought out the fact that the Standard Oil Co. had received in 17 months $10,000,000 as rebates ; and yet I gather from your remark that you are not in favor of the Inter-State Commerce law.

As near as I can understand, you are opposed to all laws that are what you call in restraint of trade. You emphasize that statement in the report. You find fault with the anti-consolidation law. Are you opposed to a protective tariff law that says I shall not purchase my goods from abroad unless I pay a duty or tax ? You know you are not, for the moment that law is removed and competition from other countries comes in, trusts in this country would be good, indeed. They would be dead trusts, for universal combination is impossible. I quote from your letter :

I am opposed to the principle that prevents consolidation. I believe in the rights of property, and do not want such men as you to say to me whom it is proper for me to consolidate my property with. To my mind it is only absurd for a man who, if he employs another, the range of employment only reaching from blacking your boots to driving your team, to say to others what he shall or shall not do.

I need not italicize any of the above, but I am sorry you wrote it, for after all the sharp and cutting things you have said about me, I have nothing personally but kind feelings.

Let me paraphrase your statement : I believe in the rights of property and do not want you or a board of trustees to measure the price according to your interests, of an article I am obliged to purchase. The public and myself have the right to obtain it at the lowest price that open competition will afford it at. An associated capital and centralized management have no right in law or justice to step in and deprive me of that competition.

SUPPLY AND DEMAND DO NOT CONTROL THE TRUST.

It is vain to say that " no combination can ignore the laws of supply and demand, nor can they form a trust that will be able to do so." The fact is patent that that is precisely what *is* done. The very purpose of a trust combine is to circumvent that law. To make the point near home, was it the law of demand and supply that closed at one time so many strawboard factories and thereby discharged all the employes ? Was it this law that raised the price?

" New capital," you say, " is constantly coming in as a menace to high profits." In the making of strawboard, natural gas has come in as well as new capital, as a factor, but it will not be long before a new combination will be effected, if it has not already been launched, to continue the solid prosperity and special privilege of the old combination. Manufacturing stock that is selling in the open market at 150 must have " high profits " behind it. I could go on and show by actual results, obtained from the testimony, that you are in error in stating that "a monopoly cannot be maintained except on the basis of low prices and *small* profits."

DIAMOND MATCH CO. PROFITS.

Let me tell you another instance, taken from common public report among business men, as well as stock quotations. If I misstate, please correct me. The Diamond Match trust was formed four or five years ago under the laws of Connecticut. It embraced nearly all the match interests in the country. The property was made over to trustees and trust certificates were issued to the amount of about $3,000,000. How much water was put into this I can't say. You can. But suppose there was no water and all good property, were the "profits high" or not ? That depends upon what you call high profits. As I am looking through a "gimlet hole," the following looks pretty well up to me, especially after paying salaries, expenses, taxes, etc.

OFFICE OF THE DIAMOND MATCH CO.,
AKRON, O., August 20, 1888.

The dividend resolution passed by the Board of Directors of the Company, at its meeting on February 1st, 1888, is as follows :

Resolved, That a dividend of eighteen (18) per cent. on the capital stock of this Company be declared out of the net earnings of the Company for the year 1887 ; the same to be paid in quarterly installments of four and one-half (4½) per cent. each, which shall be due and payable, respectively, on the 20th days of February, May, August and November, 1888, to stockholders of record on the dates of fifth (5th) of each of the said months of February, May, August and November, 1888 ; and that no transfer of stock be made on either of the said fifth days of the months aforesaid.

I have the pleasure of enclosing the third (3d) installment of said dividend due on your stock. Please acknowledge receipt of same, and oblige,

Very truly yours,

O. C. BARBER,

Treasurer.

But evidently this does not represent all the profits, for within the last six months the entire "plant," according to the migratory custom of trusts, has gone to Illinois and the same property has there been reorganized and recapitalized at $6,000,000, just double, and I see by Chicago quotations that this duplicated stock has sold at 150 ! Now, in the light of the above (if it is true—and if it is not, make the correction), how can you say that a monopoly cannot be maintained except on the basis of low prices and small profits?

In almost every one of the combinations I have named, high profits have been made on the most extravagant valuations.

WHERE THE AQUA PURA COMES IN.

And right here is one of the greatest objections, viz : The creation of large amounts of fictitious property, in other words, "watered stock." The mode pursued in creating trusts is this: The several "plants " are put into the joint trust at a very high valuation, in the first place, often including tangible and intangible property, such as good will, patents, trade marks, and the face value of the trust certificates is then fixed at a sum largely in excess of the real value of the property. This is where the "watering" process comes in. And on these certificates, in many cases representing a large amount of water, after paying high salaries, ranging from $3,000 to 25,000 per year, high profits are made. Let me instance one or two. Take the oil trust. Thirteen trustees each receive $25,000 per year as salary, and when Mr. Rockefeller was asked by the Congressional Committee how much the stock was watered, *he refused to answer*. And still the profit in one year, as I stated in my last letter, amounted to $20,000,000. It has made regular dividends of about 12 to 13 per cent., according to the testimony.

In the "sugar-trust" after the several concerns were valued, trust certificates were issued for about 50 per cent. in excess, so that 50 per cent. of the face value represented *nothing but water.* And yet dividends were declared on this stock. The evidence shows that in many cases the parties came with counsel, in some cases they refused to answer, in others great efforts were made to conceal the earning power of the trust. The property was capitalized as largely as possible ; large amounts are carried forward to "surplus account," and covered up under various names. These facts speak louder than words, whether large gains are possible or not when a monopoly exists.

These details take up too much space, but they are of more value to the reader and more convincing upon the question of the possibility of large profits than all the fine-spun theories on general principles you have formulated. If you were not such a stickler for broad, "general principles" and so fearful of details that "might be confusing," I think you could furnish some suggestive figures.

RAILROAD CONSOLIDATIONS.

A wave of the hand will not dispose of the matter of railroad consolidations. Competing lines in this State cannot consolidate. Years ago, when the Vanderbilt party came to Ohio and obtained control of two competing lines of road, they attempted to consolidate them. The Supreme Court of this State, at the instance of a State officer, annulled the consolidation.

Does it imply going back to ancient times and antiquated notions, to insist upon competition as " the life of trade ? " Are not all our merchants, grocers, tradesmen, tailors, blacksmiths, etc., in open competition, and are they not fully abreast of the times ? Would you change this and constitute the rule of centralization and one management ?

Indeed, the logic of your argument, as a friend suggests, in favor of aggregating capital and management, would give us a monarchy, or a government in a few hands, instead of a "government of the people, by the people and for the people." You, in order to promote efficiency and economy, would make it a government of trustees, a conclave of cardinals, a king and his council. It would prevent waste, secure a better civil service,.etc. And when I object

that history shows that such concentration of power has ever
resulted in tyranny and oppression, you will no doubt answer, as
before, that you are not defending a bad monarchy, or a bad king,
only a "good trust." The fallacy of your argument is that this
trust must be placed in earthen vessels, in human hands, where selfish interests have full play and obtain the mastery.

FARMERS AND THE RAILROADS.

You ascribe the depressed condition of agricultural interests,and
low price of land here, to the opening up of new lands in the West ;
out there is another cause you forget to name—the consolidation
of railroad corporations, stretching out their long arms and branches
to every part of the country. Their systems of management, regulating their own freights, merely to promote their own interests
and to secure the longest haul, often have transported wheat and
other productions of the great West past our doors to the Eastern
markets, at a less cost than we pay in Ohio to transport products
to New York. This helped the West, but farmers in Ohio, with
high-priced lands, were compelled to compete on unequal terms
with the farmers of the Northwest.

The tendency of this was and is to advance the value of land in
the West to the injury of lands here ; but I see you are in favor of
consolidation. The Inter-State Commerce law was passed in order
to prevent such unfair discrimination.

"ARMOUR MEAT TRUST."

Formerly farmers in Ohio enjoyed a large revenue and profit in
the raising and sale of live stock. The butchers went to the farmers
and bought oxen, cows and calves for cash at good prices. But
this industry has been entirely destroyed by the centralization and
consolidation of the dressed beef business in Chicago. That powerful combination has taken entire possession of the field and now
has substantially the control of the business. I don't know how the
change has affected the price or quality of meat, but I do know it
has very seriously injured the farming interests in this State and
elsewhere.

A NEW TRUST.

Among the latest accessions to the combinations is the "nut
and bolt trust." I see by a clipping from the _Leader_ that a new
feature was introduced. Some time ago there was a concern in
Rochester which sold machines for making wood screws to any one
who could pay for them. This interfered with the combined nut

and bolt makers and the establishment was bought out. Now these
machines cannot be purchased. This is a heroic way to shut out
competition.

You seem to think I am throwing "sop" to the farmers and
workingmen. Nothing of the kind. I am seeking no favor and
no office; I am independent and have no more interest in the
matter than any other citizen and don't know that I would have
said anything more about it if you had not asked me to do so.
Whenever a combination or union of workingmen combine together
to prevent the fullest and amplest competition in the price of labor,
I shall take precisely the same position. Such union or combination has no right to use force, violence or threats to prevent others
working at cheaper rates than the trust has to use money to prevent
competition and put up prices upon consumers.

Very truly,   J. A. KOHLER.

No. 5.

Mr. Barber in Reply to Mr. Kohler's No. 4.

AN ERA OF COMBINES—IT MEANS PROSPERITY.

JUNE 22, 1889.

Mr. J. A. Kohler :

DEAR SIR : I have read your last effort with mingled feelings
of pleasure and sympathy. You scold me about my style, like a
pedagogue; you complain about the length of my article and because it took me a week to write it, yet all of your own efforts have
taken the same time, if their being published Saturdays is an indication ; and then you complain of my quotations ; and enter a final
protest at it all by saying " Fiddlesticks "—which is particularly
classical, besides being very witty and funny, and it makes me wonder how you happened to think of it. The subject we are discussing is too serious a matter to be pettifogged on either side, and if I
have used strong language it is because I feel as I talk. Perhaps I
have been prompted by your example. You have classed the institutions in which I am concerned as conspiracies to rob the public,
and emphasized the matter by saying, "The language is none too
strong." If such is the case, then I am a conspirator and a robber.
If it is not the case, who is to be responsible for proclaiming such
defamatory and erroneous statements in every country school-house
and hamlet?

I assure you the task which I have undertaken is not a pleasant one, but I am not inclined to sit quietly by without a word of protest when such anarchical seeds of discord, as your utterances are calculated to produce, are being sown.

You presumed to mention in a public speech, made, as you say, at the invitation of a laboring man's association, that the Diamond Match Company was one of a kind of institutions that should be suppressed. If that is the case, then I should be suppressed. If it is not the case, then you should be suppressed. Hence my debate of this question with you.

How different your mind runs from that of one of our best-known business men, Andrew Carnegie   Bearing on this subject, I quote from his late article in the *North American Review*, on " Wealth."

ANDREW CARNEGIE SAYS :

"We accept and welcome, therefore, as conditions to which we must accommodate ourselves, great inequality of environment, the concentration of business, industrial and commercial, in the hands of a few, and the law of competition between these, as being not only beneficial, but essential for the future progress of the race. Having accepted these, it follows that there must be greater scope for exercise of special ability in the merchant and in the manufacturer who have to conduct affairs upon a great scale. That this talent for organization of management is rare among men is proved by the fact that it invariably secures for its possessor enormous rewards, no matter where or under what laws or conditions. The experienced in affairs always rate the man whose services can be obtained as a partner as not only the first consideration, but such as to render the question of his capital scarcely worth considering, for such men soon create capital ; while without the special talent required, capital soon takes wings. Such men become interested in firms or corporations using millions ; and estimating only simple interest to be made upon the capital invested, it is inevitable that their income must exceed their expenditures, and that they must accumulate wealth. Nor is there any middle ground which such men can occupy, because the great manufacturing or commercial concern which does not earn at least interest upon its capital soon becomes bankrupt."

A COMMENT ON CARNEGIE.

An eminent writer, commenting upon the paragraph just quoted, says :

Mr. Carnegie, characteristically enough, looks at the whole subject from the true profit-maker's standpoint—viz, taking the whole world as it stands materially, economically, socially and intellectually, governed as it is by its

present social instincts, laws, passions and forces, how can we make the most
out of it possible? To him the world and man, science and art, wealth and
want, fact and faith are all raw materials and implements—plant and tools,
environment and opportunity. We did not make them so, but find them so.
Life is a problem of profit, but the profit lies in five distinct but analogous
fields—physical, economic, social, moral, intellectual. Profit in physical life
means health. In the economic it is wealth. In social life it is affection and
friendship. In moral life it is esteem. In intellectual life it is wisdom. We
strive for all these forms of profit together and get varying proportions of each.
Mr. Carnegie does not elaborte these points because they are rather part of the
standpoint, from which he looks, than his view. They are that major premise
which is never expressed.

There is another principle of political economy which has much to do with
explaining inequality in the accumulation of wealth. That is, that the capital
and other adjuncts which employ a man receive from the product an average
wage or share, which remains in substantial equilibrium with the share which
the man receives in wages. Mr. Stuart Wood has endeavored to give form to
this principle by stating that, whenever the work can be performed by machinery in lieu of the man, the wage will constantly tend to equal the average returns
on the amount of capital invested in the machinery.

Contrast this reasoning with that of Dr. Barry, in his article in
the *North American Review*, entitled the "Moloch of monopoly:"

We have before us an amazing spectacle. We see a great multitude plow-
ing fields, raising the harvests, digging mines, smelting ores, building great
factories and filling them with machinery, weaving and fashioning all manner
of beautiful and useful things by means of the machinery they have made;
running the railways, launching the ships, carrying the produce of their toil to
the world's end, and bringing thence in exchange what other multitudes have
in like manner created. And then, note the magic transformation! The ban-
quet of civilization is spread and the company sit down. Are they the toilers
of the sea and land whom we beheld so busy? Do these eat the fruit of their
hands? By no manner of means! They have withdrawn out of sight to their
dog-kennels, otherwise called hired tenements, and to their festering scraps—
too often raked out of the refuse—in the strength of which they are free to
live, to propagate and to create fresh capital. "Homeless, landless, moneyless,"
such is literally their condition. They are not even supposed to get a fair share
of the commodities their hands and brains have produced. The monopolist
bids them compete, not with him, but with one another, and he stands by to
accept, in the name of equity, the lowest tender.

The same writer on Dr. Barry's production, says as follows:

Dr. Barry himself obeys the laws of supply and demand when he peppers
a congregation of holders of private property with expletives against private
ownership, for the reason that men go to church on Sunday for an intellectual
rest or change, and having been striving for the accumulation of wealth all
the week, they get what they go for when they get a denunciation of that to
which the week is devoted. But when this spirit of denunciation passes outside
the function of "giving us a rest" and undertakes to assume the form of

action by stimulating the ignorant to believe that some sort of abolition of private property will presently be brought about by force, then society makes short work of the agitator, and very properly; for the views which Dr. Barry so freely expresses do not vary fundamentally from those entertained by Parsons, Spies, Lingg and the other Chicago anarchists.

COST OF NECESSARIES REDUCED.

Combinations of capital and talent are reducing the cost of the necessaries and comforts of life, and while wealth is accumulating, so are all the comforts, many of which heretofore considered luxuries are now deemed necessaries, and no such conditions as Dr. Barry describes have an existence if man is willing to work; and especially not in our country, where it requires but industry and integrity to make a living.

Progress made in the cotton industry is an apt illustration of what is being accomplished by concentration of capital. In *The United States Census Report*, for 1880 (Vol. II, "Statistics of Manufacturers," pp. 531 to 547), showing the progress from 1830 to 1880, you will find the following:

TABLE *showing the Progress of the Cotton Industry from* 1830 *to* 1880.

Cotton Industry.	1830.	1880.
Number of establishments......................	801	756
Aggregate capital invested.....................	$40,612,984	$208,280,346
Number of pounds cloth produced.........	59,514,926	607,264,241
Number of persons employed.................	62,208	172,544
Number of spindles employed...............	1,246,703	10,653,435
Amount of capital to establishment.........	$50,702	$275,502
Ratio of pounds produced to capital........	1.4 to $1	2.4 to $1
Ratio of capital to persons employed.......	$652.85 to 1	$1,207.17 to 1
Ratio of spindles to persons employed.....	22 to 1	62 to 1
Ratio of capital to spindles employed......	$32.58 to 1	$19.55 to 1
Ratio of pounds produced to persons employed	950.7 to 1	3,519.5 to 1
Ratio of pounds produced to spindles......	47.6 to 1	57. to 1
Annual consumption of pounds of cotton cloth per capita..........	5.90	13.91
Price of cotton cloth per yard................	17 cts.	7 cts.
Average wages of women per week.........	$2.25	$5.40

It will thus be seen that in the 756 large establishments in 1880, in which the aggregate capital invested was five times as great as that in the 801 small establishments in 1830, the capital invested per spindle was one-third less, the number of spindles operated by each laborer nearly three times as large, the product per spindle one-fourth greater, the product per dollar invested twice as large, the price of cotton cloth nearly 60 per cent. less, the consumption per capita of the population over 100 per cent. greater, and wages more than double. What is true of this industry, is true of all industries where the concentration of capital has taken place.

It may be urged that the cotton industry has never been under the control of a trust or syndicate, and that the evil effects of concentration do not begin until the trust period is reached. Among the most formidable concentrations of capital which have come under the unfortunate name of trusts or syndicates are those devoted to railroading, telegraphing, and the production of petroleum. There are others of smaller proportions, but these are the monster evils most to be feared in this country. And, furthermore, these trusts have been in existence the longest, and the true economic tendency of such organizations will therefore be most clearly indicated in their history. What are the facts in relation to these?

PETROLEUM ANOTHER ILLUSTRATION.

We will take, first, petroleum. Not only is the production of petroleum in the hands of a trust, but it is probably the largest trust in the world. The worst of these evils, therefore, may be expected to be found in the history of the Standard Oil Company; and if there are any special advantages in trusts, we may expect to find there the best results also.

There are now several economic advantages in connection with these institutions that are not to be found in individual corporations. When corporations were isolated they were in competition with each other, not only in the selling market, but in the productive process also, and each one who discovered an improvement in the manufacture naturally took pains to keep it from all competitors. Under trust companies this is reversed. No sooner is an improvement found by any one corporation, than it is, from common interest, applied to all ; hence the economy which was previously confined to a single corporation now becomes a part of the process of the whole product in the market, at least, so far as the trust is concerned.

Again, when corporations combine they are enabled to manufacture all their own supplies on the largest possible scale, and are thereby enabled to employ the most improved methods of production in every department. This is exactly what has been accomplished by trusts. For example, before the organization of the Standard Oil Company, in 1872, oil had to be transported from the wells to the market in small quantities, in barrels, tanks, etc. After the organization of that company, these various methods were superseded by one general pipe line, which takes oil directly from the well to the market. There are two such lines reaching New York, with a capacity of 25,000 barrels per day. There is also one such line to Philadelphia, one to Baltimore, another to Buffalo, another to Cleveland, and another to Pittsburg, and one is now being laid to Chicago. This was an undertaking absolutely impracticable for any of the smaller corporations. The result of a saving of 66⅔ per cent. on the cost of transportation alone. In 1872, it cost $1.50 to transport a barrel of oil to New York; to-day it costs only 50 cents. In 1872, barrels cost $2.35 each; to-day the Standard Oil trust manufactuers them for its own use at $1.25 each, a reduction of 47 per cent., or a saving of nearly $4,000,000 a year. In the cost of the manufacture of tin cans, a saving of 50 per cent. has been made, the price having been reduced from 30 to 15 cents per can since 1874. As this company uses about 30,000,000 cans a year, that makes a saving of over $4,500,000 annually. The same is true of wooden cases, which, in 1874, cost 20 cents each. The company now manufactures them for itself at a cost of 13 cents each, being an annual saving of about $1,250,000.

TABLE *showing Shipments from Wells and Stock of Crude Oil on hand each year, from 1871 to 1887, inclusive.*

Year.	Shipments from Wells.	Stock of Crude on hand.
	Barrels.	*Barrels.*
1871	5,667,891	568,858
1872	5,899,942	1,174,000
1873	9,499,775	1,625,157
1874	8,821,500	3,705,639
1875	8,924,938	2.751,758
1876	9,583,949	1,926,735
1877	12,496,644	2,857,098
1878	13,750,090	4,307,590
1879	16,226,586	8,094,496
1880	15,839,020	16,606,344
1881	19,340,021	25,333,411
1882	22,094,209	34,335.174
1883	21,967,636	35,715,565
1884	24,053,902	36,872,892
1885	24,029,424	33,836,939
1886	26,332,445	33,395,885
1887	26,627,191	28,310,282

TABLE *showing the Price of Crude Oil per Gallon at Wells, and Price per Gallon of Refined Oil for Export each year from 1871 to 1887, inclusive.*

Year.	Price of Crude Oil per gallon at Wells.	Price per gallon of Refined Oil for Export.
	Cents.	*Cents.*
1871	10.52	24.24
1872	9.43	23.75
1873	4.12	18.21
1874	2.81	13.09
1875	2.96	12.99
1876	5.99	19.12
1877	5.68	15.92
1878	2.76	10.87
1879	2.09	8.08
1880	2.24	9.12
1881	2.30	8.05
1882	1.87	7.41
1883	2.52	8.14
1884	1.99	8.28
1885	2.11	7.86
1886	1.69	7.07
1887	1.59	6.75

It will be seen from the foregoing statement that from 1871, the year before the Standard Oil Company was organized, to 1878, the year before the pipe was laid, the price of refined oil fell 13.37 cents per gallon. From the laying of the pipe line to the organization of the trust in 1881, it fell 2.82 cents per gallon, and from the organization of the trust in 1887 it fell 1.30 cents per gallon. Thus, through the economies introduced into the production and transportation of petroleum since 1871, the price of refined oil has been reduced 17.49 cents per gallon, or 72 per cent., being a saving to the consumers of the 998,953,011 gallons of refined oil last year alone of $147,716,881.

WHAT THE DIAMOND MATCH COMPANY HAS DONE.

The Diamond Match Company, in its methods of cheapening production, has gone into the forests of Michigan for its lumber, getting it direct from the tree. It has invested in its lumber operations over $1,000,000. Besides procuring lumber for its matches at

a minimum cost of production, it also does a large lumber manufacturing business, and about one-fourth the profits derived from
its business during the last year came from its lumber branch.

It has kept constantly at work since its organization a corps of
skilled mechanics and inventors, improving and perfecting machinery for manufacturing matches. It is now building a strawboard and paper mill, and printing establishment, the products of
which will be consumed in the business of manufacturing matches,
and will very much cheapen their production. It is investing in
this enterprise nearly a third of a million dollars. It is a large
consumer of chemicals, all of which are imported. The enormous
amount that this company consumes in its different manufactories
enables it to buy at the lowest market price. Contracts that it has
made this year for these materials in foreign countries are much
below the price of the article to manufacturers of matches in the
countries they came from, thus showing the necessity of a protective
tariff to American industries. Foreign manufacturers are only too
willing to dispose of their surplus goods in a foreign market, even
though they do so without profit.

The Diamond Match Company can do these things, having a
sufficient capital, and it is very easy for it to do so ; but any one of
the concerns that were merged into the Diamond Match Company,
would have been unable to accomplish such results. Hence the
great profits you showed in sizing the Diamond Match Company
up. But it seems to me, Mr. Kohler, you have only demonstrated
in this matter that these combinations are very successful. The
part for you to have taken in this debate should have been, if you
could, to show that the price obtained for the goods manufactured
by the Diamond Match Company was exorbitant. This you could
not do, for in the history of the manufacture of matches, they have
never been so low as to-day.

NOT A MATCH MONOPOLY.

Again, although we are a large company, we do not monopolize
the whole trade. A very considerable portion of the trade is done
by other firms manufacturing matches. Neither do we try to freeze
them out—we can buy them out very much cheaper—they are falling into our basket one by one at about 50 cents on the dollar,
because their methods are crude and ours more perfect.

There are certain items in your last letter that seem to require
some consideration. Under the head of " Railroad Consolidations"
you say :

A wave of the hand will not dispose of the matter of railroad consolida-tions. Competing lines in this State cannot consolidate. Years ago, when the Vanderbilt party came to Ohio and obtained control of two competing lines of road, they attempted to consolidate them. The Supreme Court of this State, at the instance of a State officer, annulled the consolidation.

Will you explain, now, what you mean in the above paragraph by "a wave of the hand will not dispose of the matter." Whose hand has been waved? You are too dusty in your pettifoggery. I have not denied that such laws as you name exist, but only showed how futile they were, and in some cases worse than useless ; as, for instance, the Nickel Plate and Lake Shore cases I referred to in my paper (No. 4).

The average reader will notice stupid pettifoggery, and will pro-nounce judgment on it, on whichever side it shows up.

Under the heading of " Natural Laws Wrested " you say :

Under natural laws, such as demand and supply, the product will always be regulated by the demand and the cost regulates the price. When the latter exists, the lowest possible cost plus normal profit should measure the price. A trust combination means force. Setting all natural regulations at defiance it is an artificial contrivance to hold progress in check, regardless of talent, to create more or less of a scarcity and by that means raise the price. Under such con-ditions the trust possesses the power to fix its buying and selling prices by an arbitrary standard.

WHY TRUSTS REDUCE PRICES.

The managers of these large trusts are too broad gauge to size up their advantages in this way, and the tendency with them is to reduce the price to prevent competition, knowing that the perma-nency of their institutions can only be established by the minimum cost of production and a fair profit for their products. They make it a study very often to come close to the line where competitors may come in, and when they show their faces the price drops. This is but human, and I have no doubt but that if you were at the head of a combination you would take as much as you ought and enough to permanently bother you by competition. But men of your turn of mind never make combinations. Yet how much better it would have been for the creditors of the Cleveland Stove Com-pany and yourself and other stockholders if they had consolidated their interests and property with several other stove companies of Cleveland who have recently suffered a like fate of the first com-pany, all produced by competition and bad management.

If combination lessens competition, it also lessens the expense of competition, a portion of the savings of which is given to the public, and, instead of producing bankruptcy, prosperity attends it in which labor invariably is benefited. When the manufacturer is unduly pressed by competition, it very soon follows that labor must suffer with him by a reduction of wages.

You assert that "the fact is proved that many of the great combinations with vast capitals at command, as well as the business talent, which you say comes so high, have sent their agents to nearly every country in Europe to bring workmen here by the ship-load, in order to obtain cheaper labor than could be obtained at home, and in the great cities like New York, St. Louis and Chicago, in every riot, strike and communistic demonstration, the ignorant element has been conspicuous. It is in these places the red flag is waved."

THE MAIN STREET IMPROVEMENT.

This language cannot apply to combinations or trusts which we are talking about, and it is not proved as you state the case, and I challenge you to produce the proof. The whole paragraph is but another jingle of words, rattling together like pebbles in a gourd. Communistic demonstrations are oftener produced by demagoguery and by such language as you used before the City Council Monday night, which I herewith quote as reported, as follows :

Hon. J. A. Kohler said he was present as a tax-payer of the city of Akron and represented the district to be taxed. He protested against imposing this tax upon these people. The real estate in Akron is now taxed to the very high-est limit. Every cent of the tax will come off the real estate and not any of it on the personal property. The line is so drawn that the Hankey Lumber Yards, the Match Works, the Rubber Works, the Knife Works and all those rich corporations are left out and do not pay one red cent. The tax all comes out of the poor people who own little homes ; the big corporations are left out, while they are the ones who will be mostly benefited. He advised the Council to wait until the next decennial appraisement, which comes next year, before this tax is made.

The Diamond Match Company, The Hankey Lumber Company, The Goodrich Rubber Company, may or may not have an interest in the improvement referred to ; but if any one of them has, it would be hard to discover it with the naked eye, and I would ask you to show how they would be benefited by the improvement you mentioned. As president of the Diamond Match Company, I as-sert without fear of being contradicted by any of its stockholders, at least, that it would not affect their interests one cent whether such street were put through or not. And your efforts to array the poor man against what you style the rich corporations are as con-temptible as is the futility of your words in your endeavor to raise a dust and blind the public. I find in paying attention to many of your paragraphs that it is necessary to quote them in full, as you employ such a jingle of words and sentiments, and wind them up with such false conclusions, that they necessarily require long explanations.

QUOTATIONS FROM MR. KOHLER.

I find in your last paper (No. 4), under heading, "Statements That Were Ignored," the following: " In my last letter I gave you the names of more than a score in number of the leading trusts, and furnished you the items taken from official investigation and from the reluctant testimony of the parties themselves, showing that, in each and every instance, as soon as the consolidation was effected and competition substantially at an end, a reduction of product and advance of price followed. You took an entire week and wrote up five columns in answer, and yet you failed to point out a single error in the statement, and gave it no attention, 'ignoring' it, as you say. Now, the whole question is, Is it good policy to do this ? Does it benefit or injure the public ? Professor Andrews, of Cornell University, says in such case, if the article is a necessity, ' they may bleed the public to death.' "

To this paragraph I have to say that I have not ignored what you have said on the subjects referred to. You will please check off a few of them in to-day's paper, and before I close the argument with you I will eudeavor to finish the list.

Under the heading of "Farmers and Railroads," you say :

I ascribe the depressed condition of agricultural interests, and low price of land here, to the opening up of new lands in the West; but there is another cause you forgot to name—the consolidation of railroad corporations, stretching out their long arms and branches to every part of the country. Their systems of management, regulating their own freights merely to promote their own interests and to secure the longest haul, often have transported wheat and other productions of the great West past our door to the Eastern markets, at a less cost than we pay in Ohio to transport products to New York. This helped the West, but farmers in Ohio, with high priced lands, were compelled to compete on unequal terms with the farmers of the Northwest.

The tendency of this was and is to decrease the value of land here ; but I see you are in favor of consolidation. The Inter-State Commerce law was passed in order to prevent such unfair discrimination.

I cannot exactly comprehend what you mean by this paragraph, unless it is that you were wrong in your conclusions in your first paper regarding the decline in price of farm lands in this vicinity. You then attributed the decline to trusts and monopolies. At least that was the inference the average reader would draw from your remarks on the subject.   I quote from *Bradstreet's* paper June 8th, bearing on this subject :

WHAT "BRADSTREET" SAYS.

Some interesting statements regarding the extension of the area of cultivated land in the United States are presented in the May Report of the Statistician of the Department of Agriculture.   It appears that the area under the four principal arable crops—corn, wheat, oats and cotton—increased from 128,-000,000 acres in 1879 to 159,000,000 acres in 1888.   This represents an expansion in nine years of the area under those crops of 31,000,000 acres, or an extent of land more than equaling the entire area of the three northern New England States.   The increase in the area under corn, oats and cotton is greater than the total area of the State of Ohio.   This striking result leads the statistician to make the further calculation that, if the increase in all tilled and grass land has been in the same proportion as that in the four crops mentioned, we have now a total area of improved lands in farms of 356,000,000 acres as compared with 285,000,000 acres in 1879, or an increase almost equal to the total surface area of New England, New York and New Jersey, equaling the entire cotton States, with the addition of Delaware and Maryland.   The figures of the coming census dealing with the agricultural area should present some interesting comparisons with those of the last census year.

These statistics are startling, and may show the farmer the correct reason for the decline in the price of his land.   The Inter-State Commerce Bill has been in operation for two years, and yet every day farm lands in these parts are declining, not because oil or matches are too high, for they never were lower, and I would infer from the paragraph just quoted from your last paper (No. 4) that you were opposed to long railways.   I suppose you want to cut them up in links like sausage and wienerwurst and have a separate organization for each link.   Your system of political economy is a little antiquated for this age.   Compare your thoughts in this line with those of a few eminent men whom I quote.

BENEFITS OF AGGREGATED CAPITAL.

A political economist, in writing on this subject and quoting from others says the only hope of breaking up the separation of mankind into employer and employe, and giving the employe an interest in the business is in the extension of the combination of partnership principle, and urges that all legal obstacles to combination should be taken away.   He says :

I shall never forget the eloquence and learning with which this theory was advocated by the venerable Henry C. Carey, in the Constitutional Convention of Pennsylvania in 1873.   A synopsis of his views will be found in volume 5, page 477, of the debates of that body.   He proved by history, experience and reason that "the more perfect the power of association, the greater the power of production and the larger the proportion of the product which falls to the laborers' share." He urged that the Constitution should provide that any three or more persons might associate as a corporation for any lawful purpose. The provision was not put in the Constitution, but the Legislature of that State adopted it in effect at its next session.

Again :

Surely we are in line with the best thinkers of the age when we conclude with Prof. Sumner in his work, "What Social Classes Owe to Each Other," p. 55 : "There is every indication that we are to see new developments of the power of aggregated capital to serve civilization, and that the new developments will be made right here in America. Joint stock companies are yet in their infancy ; and incorporated capital, instead of being a thing which can be overturned, is a thing which is becoming more and more indispensable. * * * * Aggregated capital will be more and more essential to the performance of our social tasks. * * * This tendency is in the public interest. * * * We are to see the development of the country pushed forward at an unprecedented rate by an aggregation of capital, and a systematic application of it under the direction of competent men. This development will be for the benefit of all."

LAWS INTERFERING WITH TRADE.

Buckle says in Vol. I, page 277 : " Every European Government which has legislated respecting trade has acted as if its main object were to suppress the trade and ruin the traders. Instead of leaving the national industry to take its own course it has been troubled by an interminable series of regulations, all intended for its good, and all inflicting serious harm. To such a height has this been carried, that the commercial reforms which have distinguished England during the last 20 years have solely consisted in undoing this mischievous and intrusive legislation. It is no exaggeration to say, that the history of the commercial legislation of Europe presents every possible contrivance for hampering the energies of commerce. In every quarter and at every moment, the hand of Government was felt. Bounties to raise up a losing trade, and taxes to pull down a remunerative one ; this branch of industry forbidden, and that branch of industry encouraged ; laws to regulate wages ; laws to regulate prices ; laws to regulate profits ; interference with markets, interference with manufactories, interference with machinery, interference even with shops."

EXCESSIVE COMPETITION DISASTROUS.

Prof. Hadley, in his work on "Railroad Transportation," asserts that competition carried to its utmost limit must always end in disaster and bankruptcy to the trades and injury to the public. Hudson in " Railways and the Republic," refutes this view and contends that public benefit is derived from competition alone. Both of them are right if their definitions of what competition is are accepted. Hudson says competition is not merely a strife to undersell at all hazards, but that "the true purpose of competition is to secure patronage by doing more for the same money than any rival." And again : "Competition seeks to increase profits by enlarging the volume of transactions, so that a small profit shall yield greater returns on a large volume of business than a large profit on a small volume of business."

Hon. L. Blodgett says: "An unrestricted competition will not continue to be practicable even if it were desirable, because of the general belief that some sort of action is necessary to the safety of nearly every class of producers as well as the dealers. It is peculiarly a movement to secure protection, not to establish monopolies, that combinations are made. I doubt whether it is advisable at present to open the way for permanent organizations any more freely than it is forced open by events which we cannot resist. The common law is not adapted to the restriction or regulation of trade by statute. The excesses of business combination are often difficult to reach, unless the combination is formed and is made a corporation. But it is impossible to deny that we have come upon a new era in the conduct of business, and if concert of action is not yet accepted as the general rule with leading departments of production, it soon will be. These organizations are already an admitted necessity in the defense of producers against the slaughtering of values, brought about by a panic or by direct attacks on legislation. Jealous as we are of syndicates, it is so much better to have order than anarchy that we accept the alternative with a sense of relief.

THE NEW ERA OF COMBINATION.

Prof. J. B. Clark, Smith College, Northampton, Mass., says :

Events are moving rapidly. Ten years have taken us over the threshold of a new industrial era. The old economic system was built on competition. The new one has the appearance of being built on combination. The principle of monopoly seems at first glance to be asserting itself in every direction. A significant fact in connection with the change is the tolerant manner in which it is regarded. Formerly no word was more hateful than monopoly. Of late, however, our enthusiasm for competition has undergone qualifications. We have continued to like it and to dislike monopoly, but it has been with not a little reservation in both cases. We have seen a competitive struggle taking on a type as has suggested primitive savagery. It has been termed a 'cut-throat' process, and has, in fact, exterminated each contestant in Darwinian fashion. As long, however, as it is only the weak who are in danger, the process seemed to harmonize with the general law of life. The fittest should survive. The generall good atones for the extinction of the unfit."

Mr. Kohler, in your last article (No. 4), you addresed me as follows:

The truth is, Mr. Barber, corporate power has its uses and abuses. And this is even more true when integration of corporations takes place. Individual responsibility is lost. Corporations are things, machines, aggregations, and, as Lord Coke says, they are soulless, etc., etc.

In the beginning of our argument, you were loth to recognize any right of a consolidation or trust. I am very glad to see you change your opinion and conclude that trusts and combinations have their uses, as well as their abuses. It is so all through life There is a reverse side to every good. We are surrounded with the good and the bad, but mankind is gradually being civilized by co-

operation and commerce. You chide me and congratulate yourself that you did not go about with a chip on your shoulder issuing
challenges like Philistia's proud chief. ⎮ May I remark, that you
were only too willing to go for the chip on the other fellow's shoulder, with the secret belief that you had a "pudding" in store. You
say that you are here with only a simple sling, such as shepherds
use, and a few stones which you gathered from the brook. It is
written, that "King David, with a single stone, the Great Goliath
slew." But now comes our modern Jacob, with his little sling,
and his pouch full of little stones, the Giant Monopolist to kill.
No plumed knight, except perhaps Don Quixote, has ever shown
greater valor in throwing little stones than our modern Jacob.

Very truly yours,

O. C. BARBER.

No. 5.

Mr. Kohler in Reply to Mr. Barber's No. 5.

HE CITES SOME FURTHER TRUST EFFECTS.

JUNE 29, 1889.-

Mr. O. C. Barber.

DEAR SIR : After reading your letter of last Saturday (No. 5),
my first impression was to put it aside without answer and permit
you to have the first and last word in the discussion which you
were so anxious to have published in the newspapers. And I would
be entirely willing to let the people judge and decide between us as
to the weight of reason and argument ; giving you the advantage of
opening and closing. But you invited this discussion—leaving me,
in fact, no alternative but to comply with your request. You came
to me, not in a private note, but in an open published letter and
threw down the glove as the advocate and champion of " combines
and trusts," and what I have said or may say you have called out.
In other words, you " rushed in " where wise and able men engaged
in the same business feared to tread.

In looking back over the columns of debate you doubtless see
that your guns have been doing more execution at the breech than
at the muzzle. It is no wonder, therefore, that you have been looking up re-enforcements and that you bring up against me the names
of Bradstreet, Hadley, Buckle, and last of all Carnegie.

In looking over your letter to see what there is for me to answer I see that you can hardly claim the merit of originality ; for
four-fifths of your letter is copied bodily, punctuation and all, from
the writings of others, and your skill appears to excellent advantage
as an editor, in arranging and putting together other men's thoughts
as a sort of mosaic or patch work. ˙If I wished to meet you in the
same way I could fill an entire side of the paper for several weeks
with what judges, legislators and business men have said upon the
same subject and in much stronger terms than anything I have ever
said or written ; but narrow-minded as I am, in your estimation, I
prefer to do my own thinking and writing, and when my own resources fail, I am ready to stop the contention.

In the first place you take me back more than four years to the
oft-mentioned meeting in South Akron, and put words in my mouth
that I never used touching the match combination. I opposed
this mode of doing business then, as I do now, and have nothing to
apologize for, as I claim the right to advocate when I am called
upon, what I believe to be right, and on the occasion you refer to
I did nothing more nor less. Others have spoken in stronger language, in legislative halls and from the judicial seat. Why not take
Senator Sherman to task and the committee of the last General Assembly of this State ?

THE TAYLOR COMMITTEE ON TRUSTS.

You copied in one of your letters the report of the committee
on trusts of the General Assembly of New York. Why not present
the report of the Committee of the General Assemby of *your own
State*, made last Winter ? That committee was composed of good
men. Mr. Taylor, of Bedford, a leading manufacturer, was its
chairman. The subject was investigated fully. Many places were
visited ; witnesses examined, and every claim and argument put
forth by you in your letters was presented˙and considered. The
strawboard trust and match trust, in which you are personally interested, are with others specially named as " combines" in the report
made, and it concludes with a statement repudiating our theories
and recommending the enactment of efficient laws to prevent all
such combinations. I will leave this report at the *Beacon* office so
that it may be published, if you desire it. I regard this as much
more reliable authority than what Mr. Carnegie has written.

THE SOUTH HIGH STREET MATTER.

One thing more, and that is your reference to the remarks before the City Council in opposition to the opening of South High

Street, in which you charge me with "sowing the seeds of anarchy." You seem determined, for some reason, to drag in every outside and irrelevant thing you can find, no matter whether it hits the case or not, if it only hits me. It is not worth the space to mention an accusation so childish as this with any lengthy explanation. I was before the Council in the discharge of my duty as counsel for tax-payers in that district. Before that meeting the Council had laid the tax for the improvement upon the district so as to include the very corporations you named, and when it was proposed, for some reason that I cannot understand, to change it so as to place the tax on property south, and leave the property you refer to out, I pro-tested. And I now reaffirm every word I said on that occasion. So much for that. I suppose, however, that this, in your mind, is all very important upon the subject of trusts, etc. If it gratifies you to constantly make such imputations, you may do so, but no one is misled or deceived by them.

I have found by observation and experience that the most ef-fective advocate is one who exercises proper self-control and brings the light of understanding and reason to bear upon the point in controversy ; and in such cases it does not become necessary to employ rude weapons or go outside the case to make accusations.

THE STRAWBOARD AND MATCH TRUST FIGURES.

We will come to the question once more, and how does it stand? In my last letter, after frequent urging on my part to have you do it, I presented a statement of facts in regard to the business of some of the leading trusts and combines, including two with which you are connected in business—the strawboard and match trusts. And I added that my statement was based upon current history and information, and requested you, if the statement was in any respect incorrect, to point out the error. I need not here repeat what the statement was in regard to the organization, prices, profits, etc., of these combines. Our readers well remember the details. What answer have you to give to all this? Was the statement true or not? Not one word of denial. You do not even refer to what I said about the strawboard trust. It stands confessed by your silence. The buying up and closing of factories ; the advance of prices ; dividends declared, profits made, etc., and for all that you have not a word of denial or correction. Now, with that statement admit-ted, or at least not denied, why take up much more time in present-ing general principles such as are contained in the selections you have made? What does it avail to indulge in theories of trade and business, when we can look at the thing itself and see just what it does and whether it benefits the public or not.

THE MATCH CO.'S COMPETITORS.

One statement in your letter arrested my attention. It is this :

Again, although we are a large company, we do not monopolize the whole trade. A very considerable portion of the trade is done by other firms manufacturing matches. Neither do we freeze them out. We can buy them very much cheaper. They are falling into our basket, one by one, at about 50 cents on the dollar, because their methods are crude and ours more perfect.

With all respect, this looks like a harsh statement. If there are any "good and legitimate" trusts, as you claim, such an admission takes from them every vestige of merit. It only shows that such great combinations controlling a trade, or business are, in effect, most unjust and oppressive. No business tact, energy or skill can make headway against such mighty odds, and of course the heads of such concerns attempting to compete "fall into your basket one by one." And, as I said in a former letter, what are young men, coming on the stage of action with limited capital, going to do ? What in such case is the outlook for brains, energy and industry without large capital. Only one of two results must follow : Insolvency, or the heads fall into the basket at half price. And if the "era of combines" has come, as you say, and the leading lines of manufacture and business are to fall into the hands of a few trustees, then I repeat, our young men might as well make up their minds to serve as agents, salesmen, clerks and employes all their lives.

A CLOSE LOOK AT THE CASE.

Let us see about this buying-up process at 50 cents on the dollar. When the Diamond Match trust was formed every factory in the country, save one, came in under the trust, so that it substantially controlled the entire business. What was the effect of this upon consumers. Was the price advanced or reduced ? Of course a trust is not formed to reduce prices, and at once upon the trust going into effect matches that had been selling at $6 were advanced to $9 per 1,000, an advance of $3 put upon consumers (if I am wrong correct me); so the trust benefited the few stockholders, but in the same proportion it injured the consumers.

Business is organized for profit and that is all proper, but it is the system of " pooling and combining " that keeps small concerns down and enables the large ones to " basket " the property of small concerns, struggling for success, at 50 cents on the dollar, that I do object to. And if that is narrow-mindedness on my part I am willing to be so considered.

What a revenue it must yield to the " Diamond " trust to gather in property at 50 cents on the dollar that cost 100 cents on the dollar. And what a ruinous sacrifice this must be to the unfortunate owners of such property. Men do not without good cause make such heavy discounts, and when trade is free and competitors open to all such wholesale business, disaster is not possible, but monopoly brooks no opposition, and, basket in hand, it goes about profiting by others' losses.

FALLEN INTO THE "DIAMOND'S " BASKET.

During the last year four match factories have fallen into the basket: One at St. Louis, one at Saginaw, one at Grand Haven and one at Wheeling. Why were these purchases made? Were more extensive facilities needed? Certainly not, for three of these new purchases were at once closed and the hands discharged. It is very clear that these factories were to some extent competitors and stood in the way, and to get rid of them they were bought up. That is the long and short of it. My information is that the factory at Wheeling was obtained in this way: The trust agreed to pay six per cent. interest on the value of the plant and also pay the chief owner or manager $2,400 per year for keeping the concern closed. Now I would like to know who paid for these factories that were closed up? Was it the trust? or, in the end, did the money come out of the people? And who pays this salary of $2,400 for doing *nothing?* Is it the money of the trust or are the people enjoying the luxury? This is what I would like to have you explain.

" DIAMOND " CONTRACTS WITH JOBBERS.

Again, you say you are getting these factories at very cheap rates " because their methods are crude and yours more perfect." Some of these methods are quite perfect. Here is one. Every jobber purchasing matches of the trust must enter into a written contract not to buy or sell the matches *of any other* concern for six months. At the end of six months if the jobber will make oath that he has faithfully kept the contract and purchased goods of no other manufacturer he will receive a rebate of 10 per cent. on the amount of goods purchased. In other words, the trust is in effect keeping back 10 per cent. of the jobber's profits as a guarantee for the faithful performance of this contract to purchase goods of no one but The Diamond Match Co. (My information may all be wrong, but if you will give a copy of the contract in your next letter, that will

settle the matter). The effect of this contract is to go a step farther
and make a combination of manufacturers *and* jobbers. When a
trust has succeeded in " cornering " the trade to this extent is it
surprising that outside concerns can be bought up cheap ?—even
at 50 cents on the dollar ? Is it any wonder that this trust has
grown up and become the extensive buyer and seller that you say
it is ? It could hardly be otherwise. Public policy aims at making
the general public prosperous, affording as far as possible equal
rights and privileges to all and exclusive rights and powers to none.

THE SUGAR TRUST.

I wish to call your attention as well as the readers of this letter
to an editorial article in the New York *Daily Tribune* of June 24,
on the subject of the sugar trust. In several of my letters I referred
to this grasping monopoly in one of the necessaries of life, and this
article by a conservative writer, dealing in facts and figures, sus-
tains every word I have said upon that subject. For instance, two
years ago, he says :

Fair refined sugar sold at $4.44 per 100 pounds, granulated at $5.94 and
crushed at $6.12. The cost of refining then appeared to justify a difference of
$1.50 per 100 pounds between the raw sugar and the crushed. Now the prices
are $7.06 for fair refined, $9 for granulated and $9.50 for crushed. The refin-
ers now exact $1.94 per 100 pounds for their services between raw and gran-
ulated sugar and $2.44 per 100 pounds between the raw and crushed. Roughly,
the consumption at 50 pounds per capita costs about three cents per pound more
than it formerly did, or $1.50 for every inhabitant, $7.50 for every family and
$97,500,000 for the entire population. The whole revenue derived by the Gov-
ernment from the duty on sugar of all kinds was only $52,000,000,

This writer says that the sugar trust has curtailed the production, increased the cost and is hostile to the public interests, and
urges upon Congress at the coming session to change or remove the
duty on sugar in order to protect the public against extortion.

WHAT CONGRESS SHOULD DO.

The time has come for plain speaking, independent action, independent voting, and what this writer says about the action of
Congress in regard to removing duties where extortion is practiced
by means of pooling and trusts in sugar should be promptly applied
to other lines of business similarly operated and controlled by
trusts.

These combinations have grown up in secrecy and mystery.
They have developed and spread all over the country, fixing prices
of commodities, and in the rapid increase of wealth and power
they have become and are defiant, oppressive and hostile to the

best interests of the country. To make myself as plain as possible, if my poor opinion is of any importance, I fully believe that such trusts as the sugar trust "are conspiracies to rob the people," and should be dealt with accordingly.

For upwards of a century we have made great progress in this new country. The great forests have been cut down and cultivated fields appear. Mines have been opened, factories erected, vessels launched and successful and prosperous business established in nearly every line of trade ; and all this has been accomplished under the wholesome motto of "Competition is the life of trade." Under these conditions some succeeded in business, some failed, some were rich, some were poor, but prosperity was the rule, and everywhere and at all times and in every enterprise the course was open, the way clear for all to enter and compete for the prizes of success. And the great success, prosperity and development we have reached is due to this sound and natural condition of things.

A RAGE FOR TRUSTS.

But a few years ago railroad "wrecking" and speculation commenced on a grand scale, and this soon led to re-organizations, "consolidations and combinations." Then came the great Standard Oil Company, and finally the oil trust, and the fabulous success of this company in fortune-making by this method has led to a rage for trusts and combines not unlike the craze that seized the English people in the "South Sea bubble." And now we are gravely informed that we have reached an "era of combines and trusts," and that henceforth the business of the country must in order to succeed be concentrated, organized and consolidated in the hands of a few trustees, of such eminent talent and capacity as to make the thing a success, and of such perfect fairness that the public may safely trust that only legitimate methods will be pursued and profits equitably divided.

But the fact is the people have been made to feel and are beginning to understand that a trust and "pool" is nothing but a clean-cut well-devised scheme of business, the effect of which is to make the "rich richer and the poor poorer." Of course you will call this "sowing the seeds of anarchy," but your readers and mine will say it is the truth, and hence your charge about "ringing in the feud between rich and poor " hurts no one.

SOME OTHER TRUSTS.

I have spoken of the sugar trust and will not repeat. We have also a coffee trust, and in the first place the price was advanced nearly double, and afterward it lowered the price one and one-half cent a pound. Coffee, which is wholesaling at fifteen cents, is not worth over seven cents. The difference is measure of extortion practiced upon the public.

Only recently a "salt trust" has been organized of American and English capitalists, known as the North American Salt Company, limited, capital $500,000,000. Salt is not manufactured in many places, and nearly, if not all of the salt works of the country are included, so that the combine is complete. Salt is not a very expensive luxury but every family uses it. The usual claim is put forth that the object of this combination is uniform methods of manufacture to save waste, etc., but in the end the consumers must pay tribute just as they have been and are paying tribute to the sugar, coffee and other trusts.

TRUSTS MADE IN SECRET.

I will admit all you say regarding the uses of corporations. The granting of such franchises is carefully regulated by law in every State. A certificate must be filed with a State officer in most States, giving the names of the persons, the nature of the business, where to be carried on, amount of capital stock, etc., and the stockholders are made liable in double the amount of stock for payment of all obligations. But not content with this, the directors or managers get together and in order to control the trade and monopolize the business form a corporation of corporations. All this is done in secret and without any legal warrant or authority of law. No provision exists anywhere for the creation of such a "pool or trust." No public record, no charters, no names are given, no guarantee for the safety of the public. No provision is made for the protection of persons dealing with such an anomalous institution, and yet as we have seen in the case of the sugar trust, it really possesses the power of laying a tax upon the people of $97,000,000.

The Courts of the State of Louisiana have recently declared that the cotton-oil trust could not do business in that State. The Attorney-General of that State filed an application asking that the trust be prevented from exercising franchises and privileges of a corporation in that State. And the Judge of the Court, following in the line of the decision of Judge Barrett, of New York, in the case of the sugar trust, made the injunction perpetual.

When an execution is placed in the Sheriff's hands and a farm or house and lot are taken and offered for sale at public auction, the law seeks competition in order to get the best price possible. If a number of persons, each desiring the property, get together at such sale and form a pool or combination so as not to bid against each other and arrange that some one may purchase the article without competition and then divide the profits of such purchase, the law is very plain. Any court in the country would set such sale aside as illegal and contrary to public policy. A trust in business is surely a combination of the same character, differing only in the instance and not in the principle of its application. The thing arrived at in every case where a trust is formed, the bed-rock upon which it stands, is to obtain such exclusive control of a trade or business as to enable it to dictate terms and enforce its exactions. The oft-quoted remark of George Stephenson, the famous inventor, that " when combination is possible competition is impossible " describes the situation exactly.

It was not the imposition of a trifling tax upon tea that induced our ancestors to take up arms against the mother country. It was not the amount involved, but it was the sentiment of independence and liberty that resented such an exaction without representation. It is not in the nature of Anglo-Saxons to pay tribute to anybody, or long submit to a wrong. It has been truly said that most of the great English struggles for constitutional liberty have grown out of unjust exactions of money from the people.

MONOPOLY CAN NOT THRIVE HERE.

The people of this country are not Anarchists or Communists. They reverence law, and will violate no man's lawful possessions. They believe in fair play and equal rights for all ; but monopoly will not long flourish on American soil. The sentiment that threw the tea overboard in Boston Harbor and that stood by President Jackson in his overthrow of the old United States Bank, can be relied upon to find and apply an adequate and peaceable remedy.

The experience last Winter of the people of Toledo and Tiffin with the Standard Oil Co. shows what an aroused public sentiment will do. The Standard laid a pipe line into the former city for natural gas; but the citizens felt that the price asked was extortionate, and so they asked the General Assembly of Ohio to create a law enabling them to issue bonds and construct a pipe line of their own. And such a law was passed to take effect providing a majority of the voters would vote for such a tax. The Standard fought the measure in the Legislature, and one of the members from Toledo informed the writer that at the election the money of the company was used without stint to corrupt voters and buy up the election, but the measure carried in spite of it. Then the trust applied to the United States Court for an injunction to prevent the issue of bonds asked for by the people, but the judge hearing the case refused the injunction.

Here is another case :

TIFFIN, O., June 18.

At a late hour last night the Standard Oil Company petitioned the City Solicitor to bring an action to enjoin the city from completing or operating its natural gas plant. The Solicitor refused to do this and the Standard people announced that they would bring suit at once. The entire city is stirred up over the matter and indignation meetings are held on every corner. The city will fight the Standard to the bitter end, and feels confident of beating them as Toledo did. The people are taking up the fight to a man, and are ready to order the Standard to take their gas pipes from the houses. This case will be fought in the State courts of Ohio.

A friend sends me a clipping in relation to the "ice trust." It seems that a trust has been formed by ice dealers in Cleveland with the common result that the price of ice has been advanced 22½ cents per 100 pounds over last season. Ice is no longer a luxury. It has become an article of necessary use. But here is what may be called a "freeze-out" indeed. The paper I quote from says there is no alternative : "It is take ice at our price or go without."

You ask for proof of the statement made that labor had been imported from abroad. I gave you my authority before. One thing is certain : Laborers had been imported, and so great had the evil become that Congress passed a law prohibiting the importation of contract laborers. I will refer you to the *Twelfth Annual Report of the Bureau of Labor Statistics*, page 204.

Respectfully,

J. A. KOHLER.

No. 6.

Mr. Barber to Mr. Kohler.

ONE MORE PAPER PROPOSED.

SATURDAY, July 6, 1889.

Mr. J. A. Kohler.

DEAR SIR : My time has of late been very fully occupied in completing another of those combines which you think so wicked, but which it is believed will result in great benefit both to those interested and the public at large. I have not, therefore, had the time to give your last paper any attention, but shall soon answer your false figures and conclusions. In the mean time, I would suggest that *The Beacon* publish the Report of the Committee of the last General Assembly on Trusts ; and inasmuch as the said Report is written from a different standpoint from the one made by the Senate Committee of the New York Legislature, it seems to me that it would be better to publish them simultaneously and let the public take its choice.

Following the report I propose that we furnish for simultaneous publication a final paper each on the subject, and thus close the debate. This suggestion is made, as it is apparent that you have grown weary of defending the position you have taken.

Trusting that you may see that this is a fair way of concluding the debate, I am,

Very truly yours,

O. C. BARBER.

[*The Beacon* is willing to give a reasonable amount of space to the New York and Ohio General Assembly reports, pending the preparation of final papers in the discussion, as suggested by Mr. Barber. The Ohio report, which Mr. Kohler has furnished, is a pamphlet of 90 pages, mostly testimony. The conclusions of the Committee, which is all there will be space for, will take about 1½ columns of THE BEACON.—ED. BEACON.]

No. 6.

Mr. Kohler in reply to Mr. Barber's No. 6.

ONE MORE LETTER WILL DO, BUT NOT THE TWO AT ONCE.

MONDAY, July 8, 1889.

Mr. O. C. Barber.

DEAR SIR: It was your day to answer in the trust discussion last Saturday, and I looked for your answer and was surprised to find a brief note suggesting a termination of the controversy by each writing one more letter to appear in the same issue of the paper.

You remark that you intend to answer my last letter and show the falsity of my figures in conclusions. My letter is before you.

and I am waiting for your answer, and will cheerfully extend the
time to enable you to make the effort, and when your answer appears
and I have an opportunity to know what it contains so as to answer
intelligently, my reply will be promptly forthcoming, although my
time is as fully occupied with my professional and private business
as you say yours has been.

I am by no means weary of the task I have undertaken. I
was not anxious to commence it, but your letters have interested me
and I am not solicitous about the end. We have been discussing
one of the gravest of economic questions. The people are pro-
foundly interested in it, and if you think I am " tired of defending
the position I have taken," you must allow me to undeceive you.
In the language of Commodore Paul Jones, when asked by the
British commander if he had struck his colors, "I have not yet
begun to fight."

One more letter will answer my purpose, but I do not wish to
write it until I know what I have to answer.

Very truly yours,

J. A. KOHLER.

No. 7.

Mr. Barber to Mr. Kohler.

DISCUSSION RENEWED.

SATURDAY, August 31, 1889.
Mr. J. A. Kohler.

DEAR SIR : In your letter addressed to me, published June 29,
(No. 5), you begin as follows :

After reading your letter of last Saturday, my first impression was to put
it aside without answer, and permit you to have the first and last word in the
discussion which you were so anxious to have published in the newspapers, and
I would be entirely willing to let the people judge and decide between us as to the
right and reason and arguments, giving you the advantage of opening and closing ; but you invited this discussion, leaving me, in fact, no alternative but to
comply with your request. You came to me not in a private note, but in an
open published letter, and threw down the glove as the advocate and champion
of "Combines" and "Trusts," and what I have said and may say, you have
called out. In other words, you "rush in" where wise and able men engaged
in the same business fear to tread.

With your usual rattle of words you may have left a sting in the above paragraph, but what does it all amount to? Your first thought, as expressed, was to stop the argument. Therefore, thinking the debate had become a burden to you, I suggested, by a note published July 6th, what I considered a fair way to close up the same. Whether this was fair or not the readers of our papers can decide. In reply you published a short note, under date of July 8th (No. 6), showing that you had gained new zeal in defense of your position; and since that time, both in *The Beacon* and in the *Press*, of Cleveland, you have been profuse in proclamations of what great things you have in store on this subject.

I have been so busy of late, when well enough to attend to business, that I have not had time to give the subject the attention necessary to prepare it for publication. Your intimation that I invited the debate, which you use as an excuse for something which you think you may hereafter say in consequence, is about as brilliant as anything you have heretofore said. I have rather pitied your ignorant attempts to prejudice the public mind against anything I am interested in. Having accepted the challenge to this debate, you are debarred by the laws of manhood from complaint of being dragged into it. When I sent the open letter to *The Beacon* asking for this debate, I had only one desire, and that was to have this question publicly discussed, that the truth might be brought out. Perhaps I have been further prompted by reading from time to time some of your published statements on the subject.

For some months you had been proclaiming to country audiences sentiments that, in my way of thinking, are pernicious; but if you are right, and I am wrong, you should be thankful to me for calling you out in this debate, as it has given you a larger audience than you could otherwise command.

In accepting the debate you said you preferred an oral discussion. No wonder. You have a facility for rattling off words orally, but when they are put on paper, where a close analysis can be made of them, they do not appear so bright, and it becomes apparent that your statements are not always founded on facts.

I quote from your letter again:

In looking over your letter to see what there is for me to answer, I see that you can hardly claim the merit of originality, for four-fifths of your letter is copied bodily, *punctuation and all*, from the writings of others, and your skill appears to excellent advantage as an editor, in arranging and putting together other men's thoughts as a sort of mosaic or patch-work. If I wished to meet you in the same way I could fill an entire side of the paper for several weeks

6

with what judges, legislators and business men have said upon the same subject, and in much stronger terms than anything I have written. But, narrow-
minded as I am, in your estimation, I prefer to do my own thinking and writing, and when my own resources fail, I am ready to stop the contention.

Well, sir, when I went into this debate it was not with the view
of showing my skill as a debater, as you seem to have done, as
shown by your paragraph above. The question we are debating is
one of great interest to the public. I am reading every day on the
subject, and I find that others who write on the matter are quoting
copiously, with what they write, and if you would spend more time
in answering the arguments that are original with me, or quoted
from the opinions of distinguished business men more frequently,
instead of criticising me for want of originality or praising me as an
editor, you would give me less cause to think you narrow-minded.
Or if you will, when you make statements regarding institutions that
I am personally interested in, take more pains to find out the facts,
and have your figures verified by some one who has a better knowledge of the subject, I shall have less of that feeling of disgust at the
ignorance you may display in the future.

Some weeks ago I called your attention to the fact that your
figures and conclusions were false. You have had time to revise
them. Have you done so? No, but you have intimated to the
public that you had more. If they are not more authentic than
those you gave in your last effort, they will be found utterly
worthless.

I quote again from your article, under the heading of "A Close
Look at the Case." You say :

Let us see about this buying up process, 50 cents on the dollar. When the
Diamond Match Trust was formed every factory in the trade save one came in
under the trust so that it substantially controlled the entire business. What
was the effect of this upon consumers? Were the prices advanced or reduced?
Of course a trust is not formed to reduce prices, and at once upon the trust
coming into effect, matches that had been selling at $6 were advanced to $9 per
thousand, an advance of $3 upon consumers. (If I am wrong, correct me.)
So the trust benefited the few stock-holders, but in the same proportion it injured the consumers.

Now, Mr. Kohler, the figures you give here are like some of
your arguments, utterly at variance with the facts and without
foundation. In all my experience as a match manufacturer, I never
knew matches to be so high as you quote them above, by *fifteen
hundred per cent*, and the price you quote in the above paragraph is
fourteen thousand per cent. higher than the price of some styles of
matches we are selling to-day. I am inclined to think you were fully

advised when you made this quotation of the price of matches. Of course my evidence is circumstantial, and lies in what you have enclosed in parentheses in the above paragraph, viz., "If I am wrong, correct me." Many a man has been hung on circumstantial evidence less conclusive than this.

When you use such figures as a text for a long dissertation on the wrongs of monopoly, how utterly worthless your whole argument becomes. I do not wish to imply, in controverting your argument as to the Match Company, that we did not advance prices on matches after forming our organization. The reason for our advancing them was that they had been abnormally low, many kinds selling at a loss, and few kinds at a profit.

Again, our company was organized on the 1st of January, 1881. If you have any recollection of the condition of trade at that time, you will remember that the country was just recovering from a long depression, the result of the resumption of specie payment ; and in the Fall of '80 and the year '81 prices of all commodities were advanced. (They were the years of the boom). To illustrate, in July '80, the Barber Match Company bought large quantities of lumber suitable for the manufacture of matches at from $27 to $30 per thousand feet that was worth in July '81 from $40 to $45 per thousand feet. Other articles used in the manufacture of matches were advanced in the same proportion, making it absolutely necessary that the price of matches be advanced; but the ultimate result of the consolidation of the match interest of this country has been largely to decrease the cost to the consumer, and for the last five years there has been a continued decrease in the price of matches from year to year, until to-day we are selling them as low as two cents per thousand, instead of $9 per thousand, the price you name.

Your mode of raising a dust is nothing new; it is the common stock-in-trade of all " artful orators ;" it suppresses the truth as if afraid evil might be done were it presented.

In olden times new inventions were looked upon with distrust, and even now labor-saving machinery, among the ignorant, is supposed to take the bread from the mouths of needy workmen. At our seat of government it was once urged that the steam printing press should be abandoned, and when the matter became a subject of debate in the House of Representatives, so-called "statesmen " evaded the question and dared not express themselves in favor of the right against the wrong. Thank God, there was one man from Ohio, the Hon. Ben. Butterworth, who had the manhood and courage to express his indignation at the outrage proposed to be perpe-

trated upon the government printing establishment.   It is said that
the advocacy of this gentleman's convictions upon this question debarred him from the possibility of becoming Governor of this State,
although eminently qualified for the position.   It is but a weak
thinker who can look upon the communistic tendencies as they crop
out in all forms in the utterances of the political demagogue, without feeling contempt and horror.   A *statesman* will teach the truth
and will not encourage the prejudices of those not so well informed.

One of the most contemptible speeches ever made in our court-
house, in announcing a candidate for nomination for public office,
was lately made by a young zealot, who, thinking to cater to public
prejudice, stated for his candidate that he had never been connected
with any of the large corporations of the country.   The managers of
the corporations of the city are under many obligations to this young
upstart for the compliment paid them.   These corporations are to
be ostracised, are they ?   Then what is to become of the thousands
of laborers that are employed by them in this city ?   Are they, too,
to be .ostracised ?   And are only the demagogues and brainless
zealots to run the politics of the country ?   It is well that the speech
of this fresh young man was so unfavorably regarded that the party
organ would not take the responsibility of publishing it.

In one of your papers you remark, " Combinations and trusts
lead to strikes and anarchy."   I denied your charge, and asked you
for proof.   Did you give it ?   No.   But you dropped that subject ;
and when I gave a different reason for anarchy and strikes, and
quoted your speech before the City Council, in which you endeavored
to array the poor man against what you termed rich corporations,
and intimated that they were the cause of discontent among the laboring poor, you accused me of personality.   Very well, let it be so;
but you should not complain at being promptly rebuked for public
declarations of a personal nature.

Again, Mr. Kohler, you are the wrong man to set yourself up
as the " Poor man's friend," and I ask you upon what grounds you
base your claim ?   What have you ever done in furnishing labor or
in any other way to distinguish yourself as such ?   You war against
corporations as though they were a fit target for every one to fire
at.   Do you know that it is these rich corporations that furnish labor to the poor, and that the richer they are the better the pay of
their help ?   But let these rich corporations become poor by undue
competition or unjust legislation.   How soon it reacts upon the laborer !   The greater a man's genius, the greater his effectiveness
and the better his pay.   The greater a corporation's wealth, the

greater their effectiveness, and the greater the magnitude of their operations, and that is all there is of this question.

So long as profit is the chief or ruling spirit of commercial operations, people will look to improve their methods, and if consolidation aids them in cheapening their products and preventing the waste of over-production, then any legislation to prevent such results is an absolute loss to the country. While there have been some impositions on the public by trusts and combinations, in overcharges for manufactured commodities, yet it is an established fact that the general tendency resulting from combination is lower prices, the overcharge being always punished by the investment of new capital and by greater competition in the long run.

You complain because these combinations prevent young men from going into business. I want to ask you *whose* young men are prevented from going into business? It is written that " man shall earn his bread by the sweat of his brow." Is it your view that there should be a certain privileged class of young men, say " classical " young men, who should be permitted to go into business whether they have experience or not, or whether they have the ability to work themselves up step by step to successful business men ? Shame on your conclusions ! The best qualified and skilled young men will succeed the old. Combination and consolidation do not prevent young men from going into business, but it requires at each advancing step in civilization a greater efficiency in leaders. In these times it is not only necessary that they be *efficient*, but they must be *sufficient*.

Combination does not *prevent* competition, but it *intensifies* it. The struggle to gain the front rank in mechanics, business or the professions is intensified by the high standards that are constantly calling for greater proficiency. This means work. It means plodding. Every day a *little*, but the next day *more* work. The mountains are to be delved in for their minerals. More work. The soil is to be cultivated. More work. The manufacturer must improve his machinery and methods or he will be "knocked out" by the greater facilities of his competitors. More plodding—more work !

Does your system, Mr. Kohler, of political economy, dispense with proficiency, labor, methods, organization, and every law that is effective in the present civilization, and let our young men go into business without experience, and become full-fledged men of business whether they have energy or not ? If so, then less plodding, less work. Are these young men, you seem to take a false interest in, to supplant men of great energy and experience in business ?

Then less plodding and less work, and my views are all wrong, and the order of the survival of the fittest is being reversed. Do you know, Mr. Kohler, that statistics show that more than 90 per cent. of those who engage in business make business failures ? Are you in favor of bankruptcy, with all its attendant evils, rather than success in business ? Do you prefer forced liquidation of manufacturing companies (for instance, the Cleveland Stove Company— about the only manufacturing enterprise I ever knew you to be engaged in) caused by incompetency and competition ? If 90 per cent. of those who engage in business make failures, I would like to ask, who throw out of work the most people—the 90 per cent. who make *failures* or the 10 per cent. who make a success of business, even though the latter do buy out some of the incompetent owners to prevent their cut-throat competition ? So long as business is done on the basis of profit. just so long should the freedom of contract not only be permitted by single individuals and manufacturing companies and corporations, but every man of full age and sound mind should be compelled to live up to his contracts by law.

The true competition is the competition of proficiency. The greater the proficiency the more dollars. If your neighbor is more successful than you, rest assured, as a rule at least, he has been endowed by nature with more talent than you, or else he has been plodding, working day in and day out for proficiency. Hence his greater success, while you may have become " classical " and less proficient. Yet there is use for the latter, if for no other purpose, you still remain an object for comparison. You may devote your time to " gathering little pebbles from the brook" and forming them into monograms by throwing them with your little sling— " such as simple shepherds use "—into sand banks. I object to your methods of reasoning, because they teach incompetency. You would *equalise* men by *law*. You measure by a false standard, and teach the weak to rebel against the powers that be.

You think combinations and trusts the prevailing evil of the day. What have you said in all your arguments to prove it ? I have looked over your articles with a great deal of care, and have only discovered in them but one point which you have made— namely, that combinations or trusts *can*, if they *wish*, advance prices temporarily against the interests of the public. If you have made any other points, I have failed to see them, and in your next article I wish you would briefly sum up the different points you think you have made. This one point will apply to any corporation or individual doing business, and to the professions, for they all frequently have it in their power to do the same thing. I am adverse to legislation on the subject of trusts and combinations until they are very thoroughly understood, and I think evils resulting from them will correct themselves.

I have been looking up the figures and facts in relation to the sugar business and the sugar trust, and I find you very much at fault and ridiculously ignorant of the facts in relation thereto as expressed in your article. But to go into the analysis of the sugar business and your arguments thereon, would make this article more lengthy than I care to have it. I will take that subject up in a future paper if you wish to continue the discussion.

There is one other paragraph in your paper that attracted my attention. I quote the same as follows :

> What a revenue it must yield to the Diamond trust to gather in property at 50 cents on the dollar that costs 100 cents on the dollar, and what a ruinous sacrifice this must be to the unfortunate owners of such property. Men do not without good cause make such heavy discounts, and when trade is fair and competition open to all, such wholesale business disaster is not possible, but monopoly permits no opposition, and, basket in hand, it goes about profiting by others' losses.

At first glance an unsuspicious reader might think some great wrong was being perpetrated by that unholy Diamond trust, but let us view the matter from a correct standpoint. These people that are bought out for fifty cents on the dollar have crude, unbusinesslike methods, the property they transfer is not worth fifty cents on the dollar to the purchaser or to the owner. Now dwell on this subject for a minute or two in your next, and let us see what you have to say to it.

Mr. Kohler, I would like to have you answer some of the questions in the following paragraph quoted from an article on trusts, by Charles F. Beach, Jr. He says:

> We are also confronted, when considering the matter of profit, with such questions as these : Have men a moral right to do business at a profit? Is the public morally entitled to the benefit of such economies in the production by private enterprise of a given article as accrue from the aggregation of capital and the concentration of interest in its manufacture ? Are the promoters of a trust entitled to such profits as they can secure by reason of the economies incident to the trust? Is it morally wrong by concerted action among manufacturers to prevent the manufacture of more sugar, oil, or strawboard, or what not than can be sold at a profit? Have the public a right to insist upon over-production, so that manufactured products must be sold at a loss ? Is one man morally entitled to the advantages of another man's foresight and economy in the conduct of his private business? Is not a fair price for a thing morally better than a low price

for it ?   Is not a certain price for a thing economically better than a fluctuating and uncertain price? Do the politicians really believe that competition unchecked and over-production unrestrained, and the low prices, the low wages, the glut of markets, and the sacrifice of energy which are incident thereto, will better the condition of that class whose rights they especially champion ? Is anybody so credulous as to believe that trusts of capital can be legislated out of existence while trusts of labor continue? None of these questions need be answered here, but some of them answer themselves.

These questions are better stated than I could possibly state them.   May I be pardoned for the quotation !   And will you give us short and concise answers to them ?   What do you think about them ?   Let us have your views, short and concise—no rattling of words, but plain, every-day common sense answers.

There is in all of your articles that I have read, an inconsistency, inasmuch as you take a dual position.   In one breath you condemn trusts because they reduce prices so that small concerns cannot compete with them, in another breath you condemn them because they advance prices and swindle the public. The fact of it is, that you know so little of business methods that you are hardly a fit person to discuss this important question.   I am glad to see that the question of trusts and combinations is being thoroughly discussed throughout the country.   Heretofore the debate has been one-sided ; demagogues and political upstarts have had their own way on the subject, but now wiser heads are coming to the front and calling a halt, and public sentiment is rapidly changing.

The Boston *Herald* truthfully says :

What approaches popular confusion has resulted from a great deal that has been said and written on the subject of trusts. In itself there is nothing objectionable in a trust. It is merely a method by which the business of a number of individuals or corporations can be combined for the purpose of securing those economies in administration which are often *possible* in *large*, and *difficult* or *impossible* in *small enterprises.*

The Albany *Journal* sizes the situation up as follows :

Common and statute law of ancient date and the exigencies of a Presidential campaign need not be invoked in considering the combinations of capital and labor, commonly called trusts ; common sense will be found more efficacious.   The *Journal*, alone among the newspapers of the country, has taken the position that trusts are largely private affairs and an outgrowth of modern methods of doing business.   We have taken a position which we admit is not popular, but which we believe is right, and in the long run the only tenable one.   Trusts are developing throughout Great Britain and the Continent of Europe as well as in the United States.   Trusts are multiplying without reference to tariffs.   Trusts are manifesting themselves among both wage-workers and capitalists.   Investigation of the actual development of trusts reveals that with scarcely an exception they are a reaction from excessive and disastrous competition. Sugar, whisky, ice, newspapers and nearly every product in which a combination or trust exists to-day were sold at or below cost, with a profit in their sale for nobody, and a struggle for the survival of the fittest in progress that pointed not only to a loss of interest, but also to a destruction of the principal of invested capital. The demagogue, whether on the stump or in the editorial chair, may deny the truth of this statement, but the testimony of producers affirms it; and personal investigation lends confirmation. If Government should interfere when sugar refiners combine to raise the price of their product to a point which will afford a living profit, surely interference should be had to prevent disastrous competition, and the depreciation of the price to a point that means starvation for the refiners.

As combination will prevent a fall in price below a certain point, so competition will prevent a rise above a certain point. The Government has no business to interfere and set the price of sugar ; it will regulate itself. And likewise in the case of whisky, ice and newspapers. This is one of the many points bearing on the general question of trusts, but it is the main point ; and its significance should be thoroughly comprehended.

You will pardon me for these quotations, but they so fully express my sentiments and bear so concisely upon the question at issue, I see no harm in giving the information to the public.

Mr. Kohler, you have no doubt been aware that of late many millions of dollars have been invested in this country by syndicates of English capitalists or English corporations. They buy up in blocks industries of a given kind with a view to profit. Are they to be permitted to do these things and the natives prohibited? If an Englishman has the right to own one farm in this country, is there anything to prevent him from owning two farms? And if an Englishman has a right to own two farms, should an American be prevented? If an Englisnman has a right to buy one manufactory, what is to prevent him from buying a neighboring manufactory in the same line, and thus owning both? And if an *Englishman* can do this, why not an *American* ? ·

Please formulate for the benefit of the public a law that will prevent an Englishman from investing his capital in the State of Onio, or in any other State of the Union, and see how it will be received by our mother country. Are you to reverse the law of the comity of nations, and prevent commerce entirely? Please also formulate a law for public information as to your views of how to control the organization of capital, giving the limit and all the regulations regarding it, that we may see what your views are as to the regulation of combinations and trusts. Perhaps we may not dis-

agree, and can end the debate.· If we do disagree, I shall say, in the
language of Shakespeare,

" Lay on, Macduff,
And damn'd be he that first cries ' hold, enough.'"

Very truly yours,
.
                                        O. C. BARBER.

No. 7.

Mr. Kohler in Reply to Mr. Barber's No. 7.

VIOLATION OF LAW AND TAXATION.

                                        SEPTEMBER 7, 1889.
Mr. O. C. Barber.

SIR: About two months ago you thought you had said about
all you could upon the subject of trusts, and you offered to end the
discussion with one more letter on each side, to be published in the
same issue of the newspaper. I was willing to accept this offer,
and write one more letter, but for good reasons, declined to change
the order of publication so far observed. There the matter ended,
and when inquired of as I was about further letters, I answered that
I was waiting for you to answer my last letter, in which I had,
among other things, brought the question home to your own door,
and stated upon the best information obtainable, the facts relating
to the organization, management and profits of a large number of
trusts, including the match and strawboard business, in which you
are interested. That entire statement, barring a technical error, as
to the price of *"one thousand"* matches (which I will explain later
on) stands to this day wholly undenied. If you are the business
man you claim to be, each and every fact so set forth, must be familiar to you in every particular ; but be that as it may, you have
passed it all by, and even now, in your last letter, you have nothing
to say except to discourse in a lofty way about general principles
with which you began the correspondence. I was anxious to hear,
and so were the people, what you had to answer concerning the organization of trusts under your management, especially the plan of
organization, watering stock, dividends declared, buying up and
closing competing concerns, the advance in the price of goods,
the subsequent re-organization in the State of Illinois, where $3,000,-

ooo were by a stroke of the pen added to the capital stock. With all this before you to correct or deny, you have nothing to say except that you admit that the trust advanced the price of matches, and explain or attempt to explain why it was done. With such an admission on your part what more need be said to show the wrong I have charged?

Without resources of your own and having exhausted your supply of newspaper articles, from which to quote, you concluded to take time, and ran away without a word of explanation; and now, after a silence of nearly two months, you suddenly reappear in an article, teeming with personalities and insults from end to end; and in which you flounder about in your flatulent anger, striking right and left at whatsoever you think will cause hurt and annoyance. From the first it seems to me that you have tried to give the discussion this character, so that you could cut and slash at your opponent, and indulge in mud-throwing. These are your favorite weapons, and such is your idea of an argument. I am almost forced to believe that you sought this discussion, not so much for the purpose of enlightening the public in regard to the subject as to punish some one for having in one or two instances expressed the opinion that the trust method of combination was a public injury and a wrong. It is tedious to follow in this line. The people who are interested in the discussion of this question care nothing for what we may say about each other as individuals, and perhaps it would be as well to pass all such matters by, and when smitten turn the "other cheek," with the firm assurance that

> " A truly sensible and well bred man
> Will not affront me and no other can."

With the permission of our readers, I want to notice one or two things by way of preface. For the second time you refer to the failure of the Cleveland Stove Company, caused as you say by incompetence and competition. A number of our best citizens lost money in that company, which for many years was successful without the aid of a trust, and you add " that is about the only thing I ever knew you to be engaged in." For 15 years past I've had no interest in that company, and it did not owe me a dollar. I had no more to do with its management than you have had. Suppose I should taunt you with the failure of the "Warren Tube Works " and another large company that recently failed in Akron—in both of which companies you were a stockholder, as the record shows—would it prove anything in this discussion? Certainly not. In the

business of this life, ever since man left the garden of Eden, failures have occurred, and so long as he is finite in understanding
they will occur. Some become rich in this world's goods, others
remain poor, and no one claims that human inequalities can be
broken down ; and all that I am contending for is an equal, open,
and fair opportunity for all to attain the possibilities of American
citizenship.

I do not believe in yielding the right to consolidated capital and
wealth—to place a barbed wire fence around the main portion of
God's heritage, and post upon it a notice : "No trespassing on
these premises." Give to capital its just due, but no more than its
due. Capital is strong under the protection of equal laws—it can
always take care of itself. It needs no artificial contrivance or
scheme of business, by which markets are "cornered," and unfair
advantages gained. But perhaps when you succeed in your great
principle of centralization, and when all the business of this world
is "combined" in the hands of a great trust managed by entirely
competent and great men like yourself, there will be no more re-
verses in business. No more bankruptcies and failures. In that
day there will be only a few mammoth establishments, with millions
to back them and controlled and conducted by "The Napoleon of
Finance." Then the great body of people, "incompetents" and
all those with "crude methods" who now have to sell out their
property at 50 cents on the dollar will have no care, nothing to
lose, no taxes to pay and their wages will be doled out every week.
What an Acadian felicity we will enjoy when your millennium
comes, and we can all look up to and receive the gracious bounty
of a "trust."

In another part of your letter, referring to the opportunities of
young men and their success in business where trusts are in full
operation, you ask "Whose sons?" "Classical young men," you say
with a taunt and a sneer, which I understand very well. Does a
higher education unfit a young man for success in life? Does it
deprive him of the means of obtaining a livelihood? Does it place
him in the list of "incompetents" upon whom you look down with
so much commisseration? The best people consider that a good
education is the best legacy that can be transmitted, and for my
part I wish that every child you employ in your factory could be
taken out and placed in schools and well educated, and that in the
mean time you were compelled to employ and pay for adult labor.
When you ask me "whose sons" are injured by such combinations
and trusts as we are talking about, I answer all men's sons unless

they happen to be born inside of a trust or have the capital to get in.

PRICE OF MATCHES.

Again you charge me with a willful misstatement in regard to the price of matches, in this that I said before the trust was formed matches were selling at $6 per *thousand*, and that as soon as the *trust* was completed the price was advanced to nine dollars per *thousand*, and then you go on in a half column to show that if I am false in that trifling matter, my whole argument fails. What a brilliant genius you must be, indeed. If you did not comprehend what was meant, I have the manuscript for what I wrote in that article now in my hand, and you can see it if you desire. What I furnished to the printer was this:

Matches that had been selling at $6 for a *package of three gross* were advanced to $9. So the price was advanced to the consumer, as a first result of the trust.

I am not responsible for the error in type, and yet you "tear a passion to tatters" and charge me with ignorance and misrepresentation. My statement as to the price of matches, and how the trust advanced the price, as written, was strictly accurate, and if you have the wit to balance yourself on a chair you were not in the least deceived by the error of the compositor.

CAPITAL AND CORPORATIONS.

I will not allow you to place me in a false position in another matter. Nothing that I have ever said or written can be construed into an attack upon capital or upon corporations. I believe in both. Capital rightly used and employed is an individual and national blessing. A good servant—but a hard master. I am not in the least envious of those who are more successful than myself in acquiring a great fortune. A competence with contentment is true riches. Thence be thou, who enthrone money as a god. They "acknowledge no criterions but success" in acquiring millions, and measure all men, their competency and worth, and every quality, by the money standard. Flushed with a small measure of success, by adopting and employing methods of gain, conceived and set on foot by wiser men, they at once imagine themselves Goulds and Rockefellers in finance, and Gladstones and Disraeli's in literature, and with that amazing assurance which Shakespeare says comes in where ignorance is greatest, they exclaim :

"I am Sir Oracle,
When I ope my lips let no dog bark."

Such are the men of our day who, in publicly upholding this wrong, speak contemptuously of the rural communities, and rail about communists and demagogues when any one opens his mouth or ventures to question the right of conclave of trustees to compass the county and fasten the grip and greed of monopoly upon the people.

PUBLIC DISCUSSION.

You aver that you are glad that the question is being thoroughly discussed. "Wiser men are coming to the front and calling a halt in the war on trusts." I join with you most heartily in the plea for discussion. Turn on the light and the days of the trust are numbered. A few days ago, at Chautauqua, the seat of modern thought and science, Dr. Gladden, of Columbus, delivered a lecture on this subject. It was an intelligent audience, and Dr. Gladden is a thinker who weighs his words. He sounded the "halt" you hail with such rapture, in the following language :

Talk about highway robbery ! What a trifle is all the brigandage of history compared with the extortion of these remorseless pirates of our public life. They have coerced quasi-public corporations to rob the people for their enrichment. They have placed their tools in the United States Senate. They have destroyed individuality and enterprise and used their ill-gotten power to suppress healthy competition. The patience with which we submit to their oppression is almost heroic. We have repudiated kings, yet in our industrial and commercial life the monarchical principle is persistent and irrepressible. Their acts are not commerce, but legislation, and legislation of the most tyrannical kind. Our only hope is to assert our right of knowing how these trusts are formed, and on what principle they are promoted, to prescribe the laws for their organization and appoint tribunals to enforce them. Is this Socialism or—well, it looks a good deal like it ; but it is the result to which I am sorry to say we seem to be tending and to which we have been forced, not by the laboring classes, but by the large manufacturers and traders. The insatiable lust of wealth of a few grasping monopolists has brought about a condition of affairs that may well give us pause. It is simply a question of whether they must control the American people or the American people must control them.

I am sure you will call Dr. Gladden a " demagogue," a " political upstart," etc. I will not object, for I like to find myself in such eminent company, and it would be cruel to deprive you of the use of epithets. The fact is that the trust, like some noisome plants, flourishes best in the dark. It lives in constant alarm, conscious of its antagonism to the best interests of the people ; it sees in every bush a communist, and fears that an enlightened public sentiment may crystallize into some law or regulation that will put an end to the evil effects of permitting greedy combinations to over-ride the public welfare.

We are not without precedents.   The monopolies conferred by Elizabeth, Queen of England, in many articles, such as iron, coal, oil, vinegar, lead, starch, leather and glass went down when the English people arose in their indignation and demanded their repeal.

And McCauly in his history speaks of the extortion practiced by monopolies in the time of the first Charles, and it was for that as much as anything that he was brought to the block ; and when you ask me "How are you going to prevent it?" "What are you going to do about it?" I answer, that an enlightened public opinion and a knowledge of the subject and of what these monopolies are doing, are the first steps in the process of reformation—but for this we would have a salt trust now in full operation.   English capitalists, tempted by the brilliant advantage which a trust affords, came over here and, joining with the American capitalists, attempted to form a consolidated salt trust, and for months the negotiation has been going on.   But capital after all is timid, and the very fact that investigation was going on by Congressional committees, and legislative committees, charters were being forfeited by the courts, has so far prevented the buying up of all the salt in the country.   Let the people quietly submit and sleep upon these their rights and we will have a tax upon salt as we now have upon sugar.

SUGAR TRUST.

This brings me to the sugar trust.   You say you have been reading a great deal on the subject, and you have been·investigating the sugar trust, looking up as you say, the facts in relation to it. " I find," you remark, "that you are very much at fault and ridiculously ignorant of the facts in relation thereto, as expressed in your article." Every fact that I stated in my letter about the sugar business was taken from the report of the investigating committee. That trust now charges the country from twenty to twenty-five million dollars for a service which, before the trust was formed, was rendered for from five to ten millions, and it actually extorts from seventy-five to one hundred per cent. yearly on its real capital, while turning American laborers out of work.   And in support of this, I refer to the New York *Tribune* of July 19 last, where the figures are given from official sources.   All you have to say is this, "But to go into an analysis of the sugar business and your arguments thereon, would make this article more lengthy than I care to have it."   Now, if you had spent more time in explaining away the outrages of this sugar conspiracy instead of wasting your time and space on "classical young men" and ranting about demagogues, you might have accomplished a good purpose. There is not a family in Akron or in the country that uses sugar but is compelled to pay an unjust tribute to a conspiracy that Judge Barrett denounced as illegal and iniquitous, and yet you defend this trust and the plan of business that make such outrages possible. I quote again from your letter :

"Combination does not prevent competition but intensifies it." On the contrary, I say the very purpose is to prevent competition. It has no other object. With that attained it thrives, failing in that it is powerless; and in practice, the moment a trust is formed, it sets about the task of removing from the field every competitor. Take the case of your Strawboard trust. Years ago it was formed; you bought up all the factories you could ; closed the doors of many of them ; turned the men out ; put the price up—result, magnificent success. After awhile your enormous dividends tempted outsiders. Natural gas was found at Tiffin,.and a large strawboard factory was erected there by independent capitalists. With natural gas they were strong competitors. They could manufacture goods and sell them cheaper than at some of the large factories like those at Circleville. Now here was a chance for consumers to get goods at the minimum of a fair profit, but what did you do ? Instantly negotiations are set on foot to remove the competition. Meetings were held at Akron, Toledo and elsewhere. All the concerns were brought together, interests were harmonized and a *deal* perfected. In fine, you formed a new consolidation on a much larger scale than the old one. The following dispatch tells the story :

DAYTON, O., July 3.

The Hawes Company, of this city, manufacturers of strawboard, this afternoon deeded all their property and mills and transferred business and good will to the trust organized as the American Straw Board Company, capital stock, $6,000,000, O. C. Barber, of Akron, O., president. The 15 largest mills in America are in the deal, their daily production being 300 tons of strawboard. There are only five little mills left out.

Only *five little* mills were left out ! Before many moons five little heads will fall into your basket at 50 cents on a dollar. Now, I ask, has this been done to "intensify competition " or prevent it ? On the very heels of the above transaction, with a new lease for the "great syndicate " in your hands, you return to Akron and assert that combination *intensifies* competition. This new deal, embracing 15 of the largest mills in the country with only five little mills left

out, gives your body the power to say what the "output" shall be
and what price consumers shall pay. It is no longer a question of
"supply and demand." It is the fiat of a board of trustees. If
this is no monopoly, what is monopoly? As a matter of law there
is not an incorporated company in Ohio but what forfeits the conditions of its charter on entering it. Such a league and consolidation is a fraud upon the law under which the State grants its franchise to corporations. It was never intended that the great body of
consumers should be subjected to the dangerous power which such
a combination possesses to fix the price of what it sells or lower the
price of what it buys.

LAW VIOLATED.

You ask me to formulate a law to prevent this, but the law
as it is now is violated every day. In the sugar combinations the
courts have declared it illegal, so in Louisiana in the cotton-seed
oil trust, and in our own State over and over again the highest
court has declared against such combinations, and held them illegal;
but it has in fact come to a point where these trusts trample the
law under foot. The *Tribune*, of Aug. 25, in its money article,
says :

> It has been a week of gambling in trust stocks, and the selling was in
> enormous proportions. The peculiarity of this speculation is that it has for a
> basis the belief that what the courts have declared as the law of different States
> cannot be enforced. The decisions in this State regarding the sugar trust and
> in Louisiana regarding the cotton oil trust are treated as if it were quite certain
> that judges and courts would be found of no account whatever.

The whole tendency of the law is to declare illegal and void all
combinations which destroy competition. Ever since the time of
Lord Coke and the leading "case of the monopolies" in England
the courts have, so far as it was in their power, protected trade
and the public against any and all schemes and devices of competitors to unite and regulate prices. If it has come to this that such
combinations can defy the authority of our courts, the time has
come for more stringent prohibition. The committee of the Ohio
General Assembly, after a full investigation, recommends the enactment of a law that will prevent such combinations. What the
law shall be is not for me to say. It has been my purpose to point
out the wrong. I am aware that the contest will not be an insignifi-
cant one. It is no wonder that Dr. Gladden exclaims, "The patience
with which we submit to their oppression is almost heroic."

But the people are aroused and the movement has begun.
The trust has become powerful and strong. It has defied the courts,

7

the legislature and the press.   It has many millions of capital and
employs tens of thousands of men.

But the people have right on their side, and while they have
been patient and submissive the day of reckoning for the trust is
at hand, and in some lawful form or other this selfish, harsh and
detestable monopoly will go down.   It is idle to talk that the remedy lies in the trust itself, and that the elements of self-destruction
are in the trusts, etc.   That is precisely what you want, "let us
alone."   You say we will kill ourselves in due time if we go too far
in our exactions, and in the mean time the trust goes on year after
year like a vampire sucking the life of the people least able to bear
its exactions.

You say that you called for proof of my statement that combinations and trusts lead to strikes and anarchy.   That is just what I
said, and I repeat it.   The trusts have become so exacting and selfish that they spend about one-half their time in putting up prices
or in keeping them up, and the other half in cutting wages.

I gave you my authority before.   I will give it to you again :
See Twelfth Annual Report of the statistics of labor of the State of
Ohio, page 204, where the whole portion is discussed and the facts
given by an officer of the State of Ohio.   Again you ask me this
silly question : " What right have you to set yourself up as the poor
man's friend, to distinguish yourself as such—what have you ever
done ? "   Is this a relevant question ?   Has this anything to do with
the discussion of our subject ?   If it is proper for you to ask me
that question, I have the same right to ask you ; and as you have
raised it, suppose you go on and set forth in detail the list of your
benefactions to poor men, and in answer I will endeavor to show
that, like one of old, "I have done what I could," but I have never,
as you well know, put myself forth, boasted of anything, or made
any claim of what I have done, much or little.

Will you ever get over the meeting of the City Council, at
which I made the speech about the taxes on South High street ? To
be brief about this, I have only to say that I wish I could make it
over again, and in your presence.   And that is all upon that point.

SOME QUESTIONS.

You say again that you would like to have me answer a string
of about twenty questions, by Charles F. Beach, Jr.   Now who
is this Beach ?   According to your standard is he *"proficient, efficient and sufficient?"*   Is he a "full-fledged trump ? "   I may say, in
brief, that I have answered 'each and every one of those questions

over and over again, and if you cannot understand them I can't help it. Besides I have undertaken to discuss this question with *you*. Possibly you have been playing second fiddle from the beginning, but whether you have or not I decidedly object to your getting a new hand at your bellows at this late day in the discussion. You have talked so much about competency, talent, genius, skill and all that, that you might as well put it into practice now and ask *your own* questions. The whole series of questions is but a statement of abstract propositions, such as.a pettifogger puts when he wants a special verdict. Take the first question, for instance, " Have men a moral right to do business with a profit ? " I answer that depends entirely upon what the business is. If it is the business of a combination formed to raise or keep up prices, regulate supply, etc., they have not. If it is such a business as piracy, usury, gambling in stocks, grain, margins, or such a business as many of the railroads have been carrying on with the Standard Oil Company, there is no moral or legal right about it. This first question is a fair sample of those that follow, and I shall not take the others up, except to refer to what he says about " labor combinations."

I alluded to this in a former letter, and I need only repeat that a combination of workingmen that attempts to coerce employers by force, violence and intimidation, and by such means prevent other workmen from accepting employment, is as reprehensible as a trust of employers that by means equally and even more effectual prevents competition. A trust need not resort to force and violence. It can buy up factories, close them up, turn out the employes, limit production and fix the price of labor as well as commodities and thus prevent competition more effectually than by open violence. These questions are very like your question, " If an Englishman has a right to own one farm in this country, is there anything to prevent him from owning two farms ? " No, nor is there any objection to English capital being invested in this country, but when it comes here and, combining with American capital, seeks a monopoly by buying up all the salt, sugar, flour and oil, etc., there is in the country, in order to fix its own prices, there is an objection and a serious one. This buying up of manufactories is not resorted to in order to obtain one or two merely. The design is to secure all or nearly all, so as to practically cut off competition in business and establish a dictatorship in trade, and when it does that it becomes a public enemy.

ENGLISH CAPITAL.

Is it any wonder that English capitalists have been tempted to come to this country and invest in these trust certificates? The facility with which millions can be put upon the market and high profits realized is astonishing. It is related in ancient story that "Bacchus" endowed Midas, a mythical king, with the power to turn everything he touched, even the sands of the river, into gold, and it would seem that the modern trust possessed the same auriferous faculty, as the following from the Stock Exchange shows:

NEW YORK, July 12.

Mr. James Weeks, chairman of the committee on unlisted securities of the New York Stock Exchange, has succeeded in learning the amount of certificates the various trusts have outstanding. The biggest one of all turns out to be one of the newest of the family—the lead trust. It was the information concerning this trust that provoked more astonishment than anything else. Its officers sent word that there had been issued 830,188 certificates of the par value of $100 each, or that these certificates represented a capitalization of $83,018,800. Less than two months ago it was known that the capital of this trust was about $32,-000,000, and this knowledge of an increase of over $50,000,000 in its capital in so short a period was what paralyzed Wall street. Within the period referred to, the managers of the lead trust, who are also managers of the Standard Oil Trust, have absorbed the white lead companies in Philadelphia, two in St. Louis, --the Collier and the Southern—and the Atlantic mills in Brooklyn. For each of these they have issued new certificates, and increased their capital stock to the amount represented by the addition of these new certificates, but it seemed incredible that these five or six companies were worth $50,000,000, or anywhere near it.

TAXES.

Now, of these accumulated millions in trust combinations it would be interesting to any farmer, lot owner and land owner to know how much tax is paid.

TAXATION.

The evil of unequal taxation is growing, the tax upon real property is yearly becoming more burdensome. Money invested in a farm or a house and lot cannot escape taxation. The assessor finds it invariably. But millions invested in trust certificates escape taxation altogether, hence, to make up this loss of revenue to the State, property in land receives the added burden. It is easy to find land to tax, but when it comes to trust certificates, who owns them? Where are they—in Ohio, New York, Connecticut or in the moon? By the laws of the State of Ohio money invested in the stock of a foreign corporation is taxable in this State as much as property in land. Hence if any citizen of Summit County owns stock in the Diamond Match Company incorporated in the State of Illinois, it is liable to taxation here and should help bear our public burden. Does it do so? Has it done so? Let us see. I apprehend the tax payers of Summit County are interested in this matter. I am speaking now of what is a matter of record in the Auditor's office of this county. In December last, for some reason, the Diamond Match Company left the State of Connecticut where it was chartered with $3,000,000 capital stock and surplus and accumulated earnings. It turned up in the State of Illinois, where it was re-organized on the 13th of December, with a capital stock of $6,000,000 in shares of $100 each. This $6,000,000 was divided as follows :

* James H. Moore, one share ; Wm. M. Gross, one share ; Fred. H. Simpson, one share ; Wm. Coffin, one share ; Wm. A. Purcell, fifty-nine thousand nine hundred and ninety-five shares, or in other words, this Purcell, whoever he may be, owns $5,999,500 of this stock. On February following, the organization was completed on the above basis. The four first names having one share each and Purcell having fifty-nine thousand nine hundred and ninety-five shares of one hundred dollars each, and so far as the record shows you do not own a cent. On the face of the record you are not an owner and have nothing to pay, but in fact, are you not an owner? Most people in Akron know who some of the large owners of this stock are. They know that you are, or at least have been, a large owner of it, and under the laws of this State, whatever ownership there may be, much or little, is taxable, and yet this stock up to this date has not borne a dollar of the public burden, unless it has been paid within a few days, whether Mr. Purcell owns this five or six millions of stock, or whether others own it, and the purpose of such subscription is concealed in the uncertainty and mystery that attends the business of all such organizations. It may be the intention to pay this tax sometime.

The facts I have called attention to are shown by an official copy of the organization in Illinois, secured by the efforts of our efficient county auditor, who, as his duty is, has been looking up the matter. If any portions of the large block of stock standing in the name of this Purcell is owned in Summit County, it ought no longer to lie in concealment, but it should be taxed like all other property. Now if there is no lawful way to prevent trusts and combinations, if they are to go on and control trade in the future as in the past, and build up their vast aggregation of capital, it is at least justice that the burden of taxation should fall equally upon all. And if the law is not already adequate to that end one should be enacted to secure it without delay. When organizations become so vast and powerful as the Standard Oil and sugar trusts, extending their operations into different States, with no records or books that can be reached and acting in secrecy and mystery as trusts do, the chances are that unless the greatest vigilance is exercised the bulk of the property will escape its share of taxation. If all the trusts now existing and which have been so successful and profitable had been compelled to pay each year the percentage of tax paid on other property the amount would have made a material difference with the dividends paid. Our national banks pay large taxes because the law is very carefully guarded and combinations and consolidations are impossible with them, but with these great trust organ-izations it is not so. And hence the necessity for laws to secure the equal rights of all. Does this mean war upon capital ! war upon rich men ! war upon corporations ? We have had capital, men of wealth, large manufacturing concerns, rapid progress and develop-ment and great inventions before this omnipotent trust came into existence in this country. We are not indebted to it for anything, nor will its destruction and the return to the healthy methods of open competition and free markets abate one jot or tittle from the prosperity which has happily distinguished us as a people and a nation.

I have nothing more to say, and so far as argument is con-cerned I don't think you have, and in regard to mere personal mat-ters I do not wish to take further time. With the publication of the report of the committee on trusts of the Ohio General Assem-bly I am content to leave it with the people.

You say that my words "rattle." Thank you ! Necessarily these letters have been hastily written and I am aware of many defects in the manner of presentation ; but I am glad you appre-ciate my poor way of "putting things." I wish I could return the compliment ; but candor forbids. In the language of your favorite author I have endeavored in the discussion of this question to

" Nothing extenuate nor aught set down in malice."

Very truly, etc.,

J. A. KOHLER.

REPORT OF AN OHIO INVESTIGATING COMMITTEE.

To the General Assembly of the State of Ohio :

Your committee to investigate and make report at this adjourned session, on the subject of combinations commonly known as trusts or pools, authorized by Senate Joint Resolution No. 25, beg leave to report as follows :

At the time the resolution was introduced, Feb. 15, 1888, public information regarding such combinations was indefinite and limited, but when your Committee met at the time of adjournment to organize, the work of committees in Congress and in other States had given to the public full information as to the existence of such combinations, the methods of formation, and the system by which they were managed.

Inasmuch as the preliminary work of investigation had already been done, and as your committee was left free to choose the mode by which they should pursue the work assigned to them, it was not deemed necessary to subject the State to an expense, the result of which could only be to develop information already made a matter of record by sworn testimony in the investigations above referred to.

Your Committee, therefore, met from time to time, and as complaints were brought to their notice, proceeded to investigate, and with this report we hand to the General Assembly the testimony taken in investigation of the Coal Combination and of the School Book Syndicate, and with the same will be found the contract of the school book publishers, which is for the first time made public.

In reporting, your Committee have divided the subject into three parts:

First.   Combinations in Ohio.

Second.   Cause and effect of same.

Third.   Recommendations.

Your Committee find that combinations of different forms are in existence and that in many industries the tendency is in this direction.

Coal combinations exist in several parts of the State, and are, from the necessity of their product, such as affect most directly, quickly and certainly, the interests of the people.

The investigation of the Standard Oil Trust by the New York Senate Committee and by Congressional Committee, shows that four Ohio companies, viz : The Consolidated Tank Line Company, The Island Oil Company, The Standard Oil Company and the Solar Refining Company, are members of that Trust. Your Committee also find that combinations exist in the manufacture of wood screws, matches, strawboard, flour-sacks, twine and cordage; oatmeal and others.

CAUSE AND EFFECT.

The most common answer to the inquiry of your committee by those engaged in combinations as to the reasons why these combinations were formed, is that competition has become so strong and so fierce, that to continue in business in the competitive way means ruin.   That many kinds of business, because of competition, are being done at a loss ; that only by combinations can reasonable profits be secured.   Another and common reason given is, " It is the ten dency of the times.   It is inevitable, and comes as a natural step in the progress of events.

And for the reason that, by combination, a higher standard of economy can be reached and cheaper production obtained.

Your Committee is of the opinion that no such condition exists, nor is ever likely to arise in contravention of the long established and well approved maxim of business, "That competition is the life of trade," and that any departure therefrom is fraught with danger and will inevitably lead to disastrous results.

Your Committee, therefore, utterly repudiates the theory advanced by these combinations that they are the natural result of the progress of the age, or that by combinations of the character referred to, a higher standard of economy can be reached or cheaper production obtained, because the incentive to cheaper production is lessened when competition ceases.

There can be no doubt that the evils resulting from combinations have already reached a point to justify stringent legislation on the subject, and your committee suggests, in view of the tendency to form combinations, that it is but just to the producers and the consumers of Ohio, that the General Assembly should affirm its position on the subject and that it should be done now.

The most common form of combination is the simple agreement, verbal or written, to fix and maintain prices at a certain point. While this form of combination works injustice to consumers by unjustly advancing prices, it is short-lived, and because of advantage gained by some members over others, the agreement is soon broken.

The next form, an agreement on prices, the violation of which is enforced by fines or forfeiture of money deposited, is stronger, but in both of these forms of combination the principal of self-interest remains, and by reason of the fact that some one concern in such combination is sure to reap a greater advantage than another, such combinations have within themselves the elements of destruction, and it is this fact which has led up to that form of combination called the "Trust," in which all the elements of separate interest are eliminated, and each member of the combination in proportion to his share, receives his proportion of the benefits.

The question of what to do with incoming competitors, was met by the trust. Under the combination, a new firm entering the field might not effect the greater portion of the members of combination, but would effect some, and such members affected would not agree to new competitors becoming members of such combination, but by the trust the location of new competitors would not be a question.

We must conclude, that the form of combination known as the trust, is the most dangerous, and therefore should receive the most careful attention.

An examination of sworn testimony in reports of combinations, giving the form of agreement will readily show that the underlying principle of the trust is the community of interest, and can be expressed by the term pooling of earnings, or profits by competing concerns. Without this feature, the existence of such forms of combination would be impossible, and it is to this feature of such combinations that your committee would ask especial attention to the General Assembly.

The committee have considered the general prevalent idea that the remedy against trusts is in the forfeiture of charters of companies in Ohio which become members of such combinations.

The opinion that the forfeiture of charters would prevent the formation of trusts, arises, we think, from the fact that many companies chartered by this State have, under such charter, been granted franchises which, in time, have become of great value, and which in case of revocation would result in the loss of such franchise, as in the case of street railroads. But in the case of private corporations no such situation exists, as no loss of property would ensue. Some form of association would be found, and under such form the trust would be continued.

Your Committee recommends such legislation as will prevent combination by competing concerns, the result of which shall be—

To fix prices,

To restrict production, or

For pooling of earnings, or profits, and,

That proper penalties be provided for violations of such law

W. A. TAYLOR,

WM. J. RANRELLS,

WICKLIFFE BELVILLE,

S. M. TAYLOR.

No. 8.

Mr. Barber in Reply to Mr. Kohler's No. 7.

CONCLUSION OF THE DISCUSSION.

SEPTEMBER 21, 1889.

Mr. J. A. Kohler.

SIR: You say, "I will not allow you to place me in a false position in another matter. Nothing I have said or written can be construed into an attack upon capital or corporations." From the beginning of this argument you have made an attack upon The Diamond Match Company, a corporation, falsely charging it with sundry and divers wrongs. The burden of your whole argument has been against capitalized corporations, and especially against those individuals who have seen the economy in the principle of combination.

You have falsely charged the Diamond Match Company with unjustly advancing the prices of matches, and under the head of "Price of Matches" is the following:

Again you charge me with a willful mis-statement in regard to the price of matches, in this that I said before the trust was formed matches were selling at $6 per *thousand* and that as soon as the *trust* was completed the price was advanced to $9 per thousand, and you go on in a half column to show that if I am false in that trifling matter, my whole argument fails. What a brilliant genius you must be, indeed. If you do not comprehend what was meant, I have the manuscript for what I wrote in that article now in my hand and you can see it if you desire. What I furnished to the printer was this:

"Matches that had been selling at $6 for a *package* of *three gross* were advanced to $9. So the price was advanced to the consumer, as a first result of the trust. I am not responsible for the error in type, and yet you 'tear a passion of tears' and charge me with ignorance and misrepresentation. My statement as to the price of matches, and how the trust advanced the price as written was strictly accurate, and if you have the wit to balance yourself on a chair you were not in the least deceived by the error of the compositor."

No such advance as indicated in the above paragraph was made by the Diamond Match Company. Parlor matches that were selling at $7.50 per case of three gross were advanced to $7.80 per case, and subsequently they were advanced to $9 per case less 10 per cent., or $8.10 per case net, which was the highest price reached. In my last article I gave you reasons for the Company's making these advances. Lumber that we bought in the summer of 1880 for from $27 to $30 per 1,000 feet we were obliged to pay from $40 to $45 per 1,000 feet in 1881. I would add now that pulp-lined strawboard, such as we use for boxes, which we contracted for at $60 per ton in the Fall of '80, was advanced before the year was out to $85 per ton, and The Diamond Match Company had hard work to get what it required for its business in '81. Other materials used in the manufacture of matches advanced in about the same proportion, which fully justifies us in making the advance.

Sir, I have good reason for charging you with willful misstatements on the subject. I called your attention to this matter that you might correct your mistakes ; but instead of doing so you resort to blackguarding me, as shown in the foregoing paragraph.

| In statement No. 1 you say as follows : " Of course a trust is not formed to reduce prices, and at once upon the trust coming into effect matches that had been selling at $6 were advanted to $9 per thousand, an advance of $3 put upon consumers." | In statement No. 2 you say :— " Matches that have been selling at $6 for a package of 3 gross were advanced to $9. So the price was advanced to the consumer as a first result of the trust." |

Now, Mr. Kohler, you state that you gave statement No. 2 to the printer and he falsified it and worked it over into statement No. 1. I hardly think that you can make many believe your solution of this question ; or that a paragraph so unlike could by any mistake be set up by a printer. It strikes me if you would ask the party who set the type for your article why he made the change he would probably treat you with silent contempt or more energetically kick you down stairs. Either one of the statements you have made as to the price of matches was founded on ignorance profound or malice intended, and therefore all the arguments you have made on this point (and you have wasted much ink on the subject) are very wide of the mark. The facts are that the prices of matches the last six years have been going down uninterruptedly and without an advance, each succeeding year finding them a little lower, on the great bulk of goods sold by our company, until to-day they are sold

cheaper than they ever have been in the history of their production, and as low as two cents per thousand matches. This has been
brought about by the concentration of capital and consolidation of
the match interests.

I will illustrate to some extent. When the Diamond Match
Company was formed, the 29 companies that were bought out by
it had 40 to 50 traveling salesmen, at an average expense, salary in-
cluded, of perhaps $4,000 per annum, or at least $175,000. These
men were withdrawn from the road, and for several years they had
but two or three traveling men, thus making a very large saving.
The different firms that composed the Diamond Match Company
had five stores in the city of Chicago, with the expense of managers, drays, store-rents, porters, book-keepers and other expenses
incident to stores in a large city. Since the establishment of the
Diamond Match Company they have maintained but one in Chicago.
In other large cities they have also been reduced to one store, thus
making another large saving, and I am quite certain a saving was
made in the mnuafacturing department by reducing the number of
places of manufacture from 29 to 12 that we are now operating.
These savings have made the company great profits and made its
stock valuable. What of it ? Was any part of this work illegal ?
And who have we harmed by giving the public cheap goods, besides
greatly improving the quality ? Hence I say we have intensified the
competition in the manufacture of matches, and whosoever wishes to
compete with The Diamond Match Company must come into the
field well equipped.

I tried to illustrate this business in my second paper in this
debate by a hypothetical case, in answer to which you hammered
the air with a jingle of words that first confused me, but after I
had learned the "hang" of your style, I had more the feeling of
pity, mingled with contempt that you should make such gross
blunders.

I claim that any combination formed for supplying the public
with any commodity of common use can only achieve success by
giving to the public their production at a fair price. We have had
some experience in this line, and I will state it :

On the first day of July, 1883, the Stamp Tax on matches was
removed. This stamp tax had been to the match manufacturers of
the country a complete protective tariff. The expenses incident to
the opening up of foreign packages and the stamping of the matches
that were imported were a complete protection to the trade. The
law removing the stamp tax on matches went into operation six

months after its passage, thus giving notice to consumers and
dealers to reduce their stocks, which they promptly acted on, and
when the first day of July, 1883, came, we had our warehouses all
full of matches, and about everybody else had none. Thinking
that our business would soon be ruined by foreign competition we
conceived the idea of making a large amount of money by the opportunity thus offered us, with the following result: The tax was
$1.44 per gross of matches, less 10 per cent. commission, or $1.30
per gross net. Therefore, if we had reduced the price of matches
to the amount of the tax we would have reduced them $1.30 per
gross. We did not do so, but only took off a part of the tax. We
made a large amount of money in this transaction; but in the six
months from July 1st, 1883, to January 1st, 1884, there were imported into this country enough matches to last the country for one
whole year. In 1884 we found ourselves in a position not very en-
viable, our trade very badly damaged and we had to refund to the
public some of the money we had unjustly taken from them in
fighting for trade. In 1884 our stockholders received no dividend,
and in 1885 they only received a very meager one, as a result of our
foolish policy. We brought down on ourselves the hordes of European manufacturers of matches and built up a strong home competition, with the result that matches have been going down every since,
as before stated. I am very confident that any other combination
acting on this false principle would have suffered the same fate.
Our company at least are fully impressed with this fact, that if we are
a monopoly in any sense of the word, the only way we can maintain
our position is by low prices for good goods. Low prices are what
the public ask for. No doubt, if we were to advance our prices it
would give our competitors a better chance to make money, and
temporarily we would make more ourselves, but soon we would get
back into the same old rut of no profit by the increased expense of
trying to maintain high prices; and again if we should advance
prices you would complain because we were swindling the public.
You would call us robbers and quote Dr. Gladden as authority.
(When I publish this debate in pamphlet form, between Dr. Gladden
and Mr. Gunton—which, by-the-by, was very interesting, and good
judges think that Dr. Gladden was worsted in the argument—I will
give our readers the benefit of it.)
     One to read your papers would think that you were trying me
for highway robbery. You quote the following from Dayton, O. :

                                        DAYTON, O., July 3.   .
     The Hawes Company, of this city, manufacturers of strawboard, this af-
ternoon, deeded all their property and mills and transferred business and good

will to the trust organized as the American Strawboard Company, capital stock $6,000,000. O. C. Barber, of Akron, O., President. The 15 largest mills in America are in the deal, their daily production being 300 tons of straw-board. There are only five little mills left out.

And follow it with a paragraph as follows :

Only *five little* mills were left out! Before many moons five little heads will fall into your basket at 50 cents on the dollar. Now I ask has this been done to "intensify competition" or prevent it? On the very heels of the above transaction with a new lease for the "great syndicate" in your hands you return to Akron and assert that combination *intensifies* competition. This new deal embracing 15 of the largest mills in the country with only five little mills left out gives your body the power to say what the "output" shall be and what price consumers shall pay. It is no longer a question of "supply and demand." It is the fiat of a board of trustees. If this is no monopoly, what is monopoly? As a matter of law there is not an incorporated company in Ohio but what for-feits the conditions of its charter on entering it. Such a league and consolida-tion is a *fraud* upon the laws under which the State grants its franchise to cor-porations. It was never inteded that the great body of consumers should be subjected to the dangerous power form which such a combination possesses to fix the price of what it sells or lower the price of what it buys.

I will give you the result of this new organization. Prices on the 30th day of June for straw boards ranged from $45 to $47.50 per ton. On the first day of July, on the organization of the Amer-ican Strawboard Company, prices were reduced from $45 to $47.50, to from $30 to $35 per ton, and you can rest assured without con-ditions change very much from what they are now, prices will go no higher. Can the public grumble at this reduction? You may want to know why we are enabled to reduce prices so much. It is simply the old story ; under the old regime there were maintained in the city of New York alone eight different stores for the sale and distri-bution of boards, and in other large cities about the same propor-tion, and we are now serving the consumer equally as well with the expense of only one store in each city, and in some instances we have dispensed with them altogether. We will now manufacture the boards where they can be manufactured the cheapest, shutting up those mills where we are obliged to pay a high price for straw and fuel. If it were not for calling out another tirade of abuse from you I would like very much to have you explain yourself in one matter, namely: How the five little heads, as you have pleased to express yourself, can drop into the basket provided we keep the price of boards up, or advance them? Then they might prosper. But of course you would then, as before, say that we were swindling the public with our unholy monopoly. Now that we have reduced the price to serve the public with our improved methods, you step over

onto the other side of the stage, like Poo Baw in the play of Mikado,
and tell the public how we have decapitated the five little mills. In
every article you have written you have taken this dual position
with yourself. Any ordinary mind grasps the situation at once, that
there are economic reasons for these combinations or they would
not be made, and the men managing these manufacturing corporations are not "Napoleons of Finance," as you term them, but are
quite as honest men as you, and are so estimated where they are
known. They do not go into these combinations with a view of
swindling the public, but to take advantage of the economies that
are so self-evident to them. They are usually managed by men who
have made a success of business and have a just claim to integrity.

You have mentioned twice in this debate Lord Coke. Well, *good*
Lord Coke may have been authority 300 years ago, when he lived,
but what did good Lord Coke know about base ball, or lawn tennis,
or electricity, or steam, or any of the modern ways of doing business ? It strikes me conditions have changed somewhat since then.
I have been looking up his record, and I refer you to the " Ency-
clopedia Britannica " on the subject. He seems to have been some ·
what of a crank and not always *very good* Lord Coke. For my part,
I would much rather have an umpire of the present age.

In speaking of the consolidation of the 15 largest mills in the
country you say :

This gives your body the power to say what the output shall be and what
the consumer shall pay. It is no longer a question of supply and demand, it is
a fiat of a board of trustees. If this is no monopoly, what is monopoly?

How these words jingle in view of the fact that the output will
be sufficient to supply the demand, and the fiat of that terrible
board of directors has put the price down from $47 per ton to $35,
and how terrible all these corporations who sold out to the new corporation or American Strawboard Company would feel if their
charters were made void by the act. I have no doubt the Portage
Strawboard Company would mourn a good deal over the subject,
as they no longer have any use for the charter, and all the other
corporations no doubt would be in mourning over such a dire
result.

I asked you to formulate a law which you would pronounce just
regarding these corporations ; instead of which you give us the profound suggestion that " the law as it is now is violated every day."
What a profound suggestion ! What law is violated ? Is there any
law in the State of Ohio that prevents a corporation from selling its
property, rights or franchise to another corporation, or person, or

company? If there is, please name it, and tell us where it can be found. The Diamond Match Company or American Strawboard Company are in no sense of the word a trust, but they are corporations doing business under the corporate laws of the State of Illinois, and have a legal existence. They are formed for legitimate purposes, and are not violating any of the rights of the public. Your long dissertation on stock gambling in no sense of the word applies to the companies I represent, and I cannot see the connection they have with the companies named against which you seem to have a particular antipathy.   .

By-the-by, Mr. Kohler, that is a very pretty little mythological story you have related about Bacchus who endowed Midas, a mythical king, with the power to turn everything he touched, even the sands of the river, into gold. It almost equals the story of the "little sling such as simple shepherds use," and your power of imagination after reading these mythological stories has no doubt led you to mythological conclusions as to trusts; and after all the slang that you have uttered in your article, your closing quotation of poetry seems very neat indeed. " Nothing extenuate, nor aught set down in malice."

Yet there is a fitness in the quotation; these words were put into the mouth of Othello, by the immortal bard Shakespeare. They were words of lamentation. Othello, a man of noble mind, had done much good to the State. He was a great "captain." While it doth not apper that he had been a member of the General Assembly, or Attorney-General, he was much honored. Iago, a devil incarnate, prompted by jealously of Othello, whom he hated, poisoned his mind by insinuations most loathsome, until he was wrought up to do a most foul and bloody murder. Subsequently Iago was unmasked and Othello discovered his terrible wrong ; and in his appeal to those who were to write his biography he uttered the words you have quoted, and, stung with remorse, he then committed suicide. I hope you will not do likewise.

You say—

The evil of unequal taxation is growing. The tax on real property is yearly becoming more burdensome. Money invested in a farm or house and lot cannot escape taxation. The assessor finds it invariably but millions invested in trust certificates escape taxation alltogether. Hence to make up this loss of revenue to the State, property in lands receives the added burden.

And then you go on with some slang and false conclusions. I would ask you again, if a certificate of stock is anything more than the certificate of ownership or deed of ownership in a stock company? The property of the stock company is taxed. Do you propose in your honorable system of equal taxation to also tax the deed of the farm or the deed as represented in the certificate? It is this kind of demagoguery that is putting the State of Ohio to great disadvantage. Millions of dollars of capital have been withdrawn from the State of Ohio because of her unjust tax laws. People have found it cheaper to remove to States where equal taxation, as you call it, prevails, rather than be burdened by such unjust taxation as you suggest, and the tax-payers, not only of Summit County, but of the whole State, are interested in this matter, but their interest lies in righting the wrong of taxing first the real property and then taxing the deed of it besides, if they wish to retain in the State capital that could be justly taxed.

Again, the Fourteenth Amendment to the Constitution of the United States provides that there be no discrimination between citizens under the law. Therefore, why should the stock of a so-called foreign corporation—that is to say, the stock of a company of some other State of the Union—be taxed and the stock of a domestic corporation be exempted? Are we to build commercial fences between the States and become Mexicanized, that a few demagogues may show how much they can do against capital to frustrate its owners? There is no more justice in taxing the stock of a so-called foreign corporation than there would be in taxing a deed of a farm in this State, because the farm might be located over the line in Indiana.

The half column more or less of balderdash that you have published about the ownership of the Diamond Match Company stock and so forth, falls very flat when it is thoroughly understood; but I do not know as I am obliged to follow up your argument and silly conclusions, and I will drop that matter just where it is, as it has no bearing on the question of trusts or combinations.

Mr. Kohler, I want to inform you that wherever I have used the word "classical" I have done so to remind you of your insult to me No. 1, in which, in response to my letter asking for this debate, you misquoted a part of it, and dubbed it as being *classical.* I had no intention whatever of disparaging the efforts of your sons in getting a classical education, if that is what they are after. I made up my mind, after reading your acceptance of the debate, that I would use the word "classical" through it wherever I could, and if possible make you disgusted with your first insult. I could go over your papers and pick out insult after insult, but I defy you to point to anything of mine that can be construed as such, unless it was made in response to some insult that you had given me. You have covered up some of your personalities very deftly, but they have left a greater or less sting, and I in turn have openly gone for your mistakes, not like a word-coward, but in language that could be understood. I am free to confess that it would have been better for both of us to have confined ourselves strictly to the argument, but it is so natural, you know, to retort when you have been prodded.

Your philanthropic wish that "every child employed in your factory could be taken out and placed in school and well educated" is another insult. One would think from this quotation that we were employing only children. We employ none younger than the law permits, nor younger than the writer himself first entered the match factory to work, and I am pleased to say it is a source of great gratification to me that we are enabled to give employment to so many young people as we do, and what is more, the most of them have a good common school education. It is also a source of great satisfaction to me to know that those who have our manufacturing interests in charge all commenced young in the business. The superintendent of our company graduated in the manufacture of matches, commencing his studies in that line by making boxes when only 12 years old. We employ none so young as that now. Do not waste your sympathy on these people, Mr. Kohler; they stand a much better chance of getting an honest living than those who were born with a silver spoon in their mouths, to use an old homily. And again, intellectual alertness, the source of wonderful power, whether applied to mechanics or learning, is not confined to a classical education.

We have children, as you call them, in our factory, the peers of your own sons in energy and ability, that will give them a lively race in the battle of life. They may be deprived of the classics, but they will have much common sense in their education, and will know how to apply their learning, and while your sons may be veritable Daniel Websters, some of these children may be Edisons.

Again, you had some other thought in view when you made your illustration. You wanted to sting some one. Now, will you suggest just when a child should be taught to earn its own bread? Have you some new views on this question that affects trusts more than other companies doing business? Or, were your thoughts prompted by the rankest kind of demagoguery? You seem to seek sympathy in this debate, and are plodding around in the dark swinging your arms right and left to create a commotion that you may get it.   8

I quote again from your last effort as follows :

You call for proof of my statement that combinations and trusts lead to strikes and anarchy. This is just what I said, and I repeat it, that trusts have become so exacting and selfish that they spend half their time putting up prices, and the other half in cutting wages.

It seems to me you are getting very desperate in your assertions, and I want to say to you that you have no proof, whatever, that such is the case, and you know it. Had you any proof, you would have produced it right promptly, and your reference to Sec. 12, Annual Report of the Statistics of Labor of the State of Ohio, page 204, is very thin evidence when analyzed, and you again affirm that your speech to the City Council, wherein you tried to array the poor man against what you style rich corporations, was right, and that you would like to make it over in my presence. No, thank you, I do not care to hear you make such a speech. It was too disgusting, as many prominent men of the city have said to me.

Under the head of "Some Questions," you show that you are not satisfied with your slurs at me ; but with a high and lofty air you ask, "Who is Chas. F. Beach, Jr.?" May I answer, he is a gentleman who has asked some very pertinent questions. He seems to be a man of some brains, to say the least, as you will see if you will read his paper entitled "Facts about Trusts," ·published in the *Forum*, September number. You will find him proficient, efficient and sufficient, to keep even your colossal brain active, if you answer his questions and arguments. He may be a new man, but he is a man of the present tense, and not a "has been."

One of the meanest insults you have put on me in this argument is that I have not written the papers I have signed, or words to that effect, or that I have been talking to the public second handed. Let me say to you, Mr. Kohler, that not one sentence that I have signed has been inspired or written by anybody else, except such as I have duly accredited by quotation marks. Can you say the same? I feel this sting, and at the same time feel a little ashamed to make the explanation, but dislike to let it stand without denying the charge.

For a man who starts out in the argument with such a high and lofty air as you, I think your last paper is a great let-down, and I have wondered if you have read it over since it got cold. I would like to size it up as it deserves, but in this paper I am somewhat under obligations to treat you like a gentleman. For further particulars, see pamphlet, which will be printed in due time.

Very truly yours,

O. C. BARBER.

A LECTURE AND DEBATE ON TRUSTS,

WITH OTHER PAPERS.

TRUSTS.

A LECTURE DELIVERED IN THE HALL OF PHILOSOPHY,
AT CHAUTAUQUA, N. Y.,

By Mr. GEORGE GUNTON,

Of New York, Saturday, August 24, 1889.

I am grateful to the president for the statement he has made concerning my relation to this subject. I saw something in a news-paper which was tantamount to saying that I came here somewhat in the relation of an attorney for the Standard Oil Company, which is an entire mistake.

If there is any excuse why an institution should exist, it should be for the best interests of the community ; and when it serves the best interests of the community it must promote the moral, social, and political condition of the great mass of the people ; and there-fore in considering the question of the trusts, that is the aspect under which they ought to be examined. I may say, however, that in discussing economic questions, I take a rather different view from what is generally found in the text-books ; and I am espec-ially glad, even under circumstances like these, to come to Chau-tauqua, because I regard Chautauqua as a departure from the or-thodox methods of education ; it is a feature of the last half of the nineteenth century, and the Chautauqua methods and elements want extending specifically to political economy, or, as I prefer to call

it, social economics. For the last two years I have been endeavor-
ing to establish in New York in a small way an economic Chautauqua, rather in imitation of this. We have for the last four years
had classes considering specifically this question, in connection
mostly with the churches ; and I want to say, in passing, that in the
course of lectures at the Rev. Heber Newton's church, last winter,
there were over 200 who attended the twenty-six lectures, and fully
one-half of them were women. And at the close, when we had an
informal examination, the women passed better than the men.

It seems to me that the question of economics to-day is very
much in the position that astronomy was in the sixteenth century.
Prior to and since the time of Adam Smith we have considered the
whole subject of political economy from the standpoint of wealth.
Wealth had been the center around which everything had been
made to revolve. Wealth has been that to which man has been regarded as the instrument to contribute. Now, I venture to take
some exceptions to that position. I ask that the standpoint of observation be changed, and that we have man as the center ; and
that all social and economic phenomena shall be regarded as re-
volving around man, for man, and that wealth shall be regarded as
serving man, and not man as serving wealth. The greatest extravagance of all extravgance is the waste of human beings.

There is no economy in saving wealth at the expense of man.
When I say "man" I do not mean Rockefeller or Gould, I mean the
masses, and by the masses I mean the laboring classes, because
they are society, they are the great bulk of humanity, and anything
that enters into the consideration of sociological subjects must l.e
considered in relation to the mass of the community. Anything
that does not contribute to that is not promoting civilization.
Therefore, I think that if trusts can be considered from that standpoint, and if they are found guilty of being inimical to the interests
of the community, I would vote them out of existence. [Applause.]

But I ask that before you vote you suspend your prejudice a
little, that you act as jurors as fairly as the social atmosphere by
which you are surrounded, which is surcharged with such a clamor
against concentrating capital ; that you divest yourself from that
influence for an hour this morning and we will see how the case
stands from this standpoint, from the standpoint of the largest and
highest and deepest and broadest interests of humanity and of
civilization.

A gentleman of the press said to me this morning, " They put
up prices ; is that right ? They conspire to simply get a monopoly

and limit production,; is that right? They want to make a corner; is that right?" No! None of these things are right. But do they do it? I submit that this is not a question of sentiment; this is a question of facts and reason, a question of science. Mere sentiment can no longer deal with the social problem. And I submit that whoever undertakes the position of a public teacher, especially upon this subject, he is bound by all the moral force that surrounds the responsibility of influencing public opinion to inform himself of the facts in the case.

Are such charges true? is the first question. The next is, What is the necessary or natural tendency of this movement of capital? I was announced, I believe, to speak to a lecture that had been delivered upon the subject of the trust, but, unfortunately, I have not been able to find a scrap of what he said; I cannot find a man who knows, or a line of print; so I will certainly be excused from dealing with any specific statement he has made. But I have perused some of his other lectures and have found that I differ from much of what he said; and in much of what he said on the factory system I agree with him. I agree with the conclusion that he arrives at that it was come to stay. But has it come to stay as an evil? Has it come to stay as the concentration of capital? Has the concentration of capital come to stay as an evil, as a pest, from which we cannot eliminate the bad? If that be true that the progress of society is giving us evil, and that the evils have come to stay, then we may all wish that progress were not. And we may well all wish to go back to the days of the log cabin and homespun and sixteen hours a day, and all that associated with the life of semi-barbarism of the past.

First, then, what is the natural tendency of the concentration of capital? What is the natural tendency of corporations? And, therefore, what is the natural tendency of trusts socially? Now, I want to ask you first to consider the question of capital for a moment, and I don't want to be too abstruse. We are constantly in the attitude of regarding the concentration of wealth as an evil. We assume that attitude towards it almost unconsciously. I want to ask you to remember that there are two kinds of wealth in the community. The aggregate of wealth really takes two forms; one form is that which is prepared for our personal consumption— clothes, furniture, literature, art—all that we consume or that we can consume, and which enters into our social and domestic life. That is, whatever of that class of wealth there is in the community only benefits the community in proportion as everybody gets some

of it—coats and dresses and bonnets, carpets and upholstered furniture, books and pictures, only benefit the community in proportion
as the community gets direct hold of them.   The refining and cul-
tivating influence of art only helps to elevate in proportion as it
touches every individual in the community.   Then that kind of
wealth should be diffused as much as possible.   That kind of wealth
civilization demands that everybody should have the maximum of.
When that kind of wealth is concentrated in a few hands it only
benefits those who possess it.   The influence of a book affects those
who read it, and the influence of a picture those who see it.   But
now, to the other kind of wealth – capital, productive wealth.
That is an entirely different kind of wealth ; that is to say, it fills
an entirely different social function.   Capital gratifies no desires.
It helps nothing, nobody, except as it fills the function of capital.
The function of capital is to produce more wealth—that is the only
function it fills.   The Erie railroad is not worth a penny to the
owners nor to the community except as it will carry us, and freight,
easily and cheaply.   The only function it fills is doing things.   It
is an instrument, and an instrument only.   It is a tool, and the tool
is only of any service when it is used as a tool.   Therefore, what
is the relation of the community to a tool—to tools in general?
Why, simply this, my friends : that it shall do its work the best and
the cheapest ; that it shall do the most, and do it the best, and do
it the easiest ; that it shall supply the community with what it needs
better than it could under any other conditions.   That is all the
interest the community has in the use of tools.   If I have a shoe
factory, what interest have you in my factory ?   Your interest is
that my shoes shall be good and cheap and that is your only interest.   My interest is that the concern should be profitable, but its
profitableness depends on your consuming my shoes, and if I do
not make my shoes good and cheap, and you do not consume them,
then the instruments are nothing to me, as they are to you.   Therefore, there is a distinct fundamental difference in the interests of
the community in these two classes of wealth.

    We have a direct interest in the maximum distribution and dif-
fusion of consumable wealth ; we have an interest in the productive
wealth only that it should be used under the most productive circumstances.   If it is better that the 12,000 millions of dollars in the
productive interests of the country should be in the hands of 12,000
millions of individuals, or one thousand millions of individuals, or
in the hands of the government, then where it will be the most effective, that is where we want it to be, and nowhere else.

Now, then, if that be true, the next question is, where is the most effective. Any one who has paid the slightest attention to this subject knows that capital—that is, that tools, that machinery, that use of the natural forces, are always the most effective when they are the most concentrated. If you should, to-day, take the amount invested in transportation, and put the same amount of money back into stage coaches, it would not serve you ; if you every one had a stage coach of your own it would not serve you : it would cost you more than twenty times as much if they were to supply you with vehicles free. Concentration is the only means of increasing effectiveness in the use of natural forces.

Now, another question enters ; and here is a question, probably the most serious for you to consider here : as it is certainly the question to which the lecturer to whom I have referred has called your attention the most prominently, namely, granting that the concentration of capital can produce wealth cheaper—that is, to give it to the community cheaper—then, even if it does, there is still another question. What is its effect upon those who participate in it, morally and socially ? He takes the position, as do many authors, that the laborer loses his individuality as a producer ; and that he loses his freedom as a social factor. That is a very serious truth— if it be true—which it certainly is, in the first place, that the concentration of capital is to de-individualize the laborer; that is to say, that it makes him the fractional part of a man so far as producing is concerned. A shoemaker now makes the 1-67th part of a shoe. He is, indeed, a helpless man, if he is turned out into the world, he cannot earn his living. That is true. He can only work when the other sixty-seven men work. He is a fractional part of a producer. That is true of other industries.

And now a question arises here, and I have no doubt it is the one on which your mind has centered. Is that a disadvantage ? Is it a disadvantage socially ? Is not the progress of society towards more freedom for the individual ? I agree that it is. I hold that no progress in the movement of society is progress if it does not emphasize and distinguish more clearly the individuality of the individual, or the social unit in the community. Now, how do these two things fit ? Here is something which nearly all who have discussed this question have overlooked. However, this is a point which is very largely overlooked, the divergence of the two movements in society that has taken place at this point. What do we

want? We want that manhood should increase, that his social
character should be rounded out, that is the movement we want.
What is the movement we don't want ? I would have no interest in
the increase of his power as an animal, a muscular man. Progress
in society consists in doing, minimizing the doing, maximizing the
being. Nothing increases the social condition of society which
does not enable man to live by doing less and having more ? When
you enable a man to make shoes by one-half the effort by simply
driving a peg, or putting on a heel, instead of stretching and sewing
and binding all day, you have made him less of an animal, less of a
machine. You have made him less of a shoemaker, but you have
made him more of a man-maker. Every time you take from him
the necessity of doing, you increase his power to have, to be. And
nothing is progress except that which increases man's power to have
and to be, not to do. The ultimate of doing is to have, to be. The
doing always wants minimizing.

If you will think for one moment, and let your eye run back
you will find this : Just in proportion as a man is a doer, he dimin-
ishes as a social man. Just as a man has to furnish forces in production, he supplies less for society and for consumption. Just as
we go back into barbarism the man is perfect who can make his
plow or his coat. But whenever you find a man who does all that
himself, I will guarantee that you will find a man who has very little.
He who does it all himself, spends his life in the doing, and hath
but little for it. What we want, therefore, is to be sure that the
two movements take place in society, to be sure that the productive
energy of men shall be de-individualized ; that it be minimized,
and what a man does should be the smallest possible, and what he
is, the greatest possible.

Now another fact always accompanies that ; we cannot have
the one without the other. The accompaniment of the de-individualization of the producer, the annihilation, if you will, of the individual man who makes the shoe, or makes the watch, is this:
When a shoemaker makes his shoes, he is a little world to himself,
almost. He has no especial interest in his neighbor, and plods
along individually. But when he only drives a peg or cuts a sole,
his very life is bound up with the lives of sixty-five others. His
social life is interwoven with his fellow-men ; and what we want in
society is to increase the inter-dependence of man upon man, that
the brotherhood of man may extend. We are mutually dependent.
He becomes our brother, and the brotherhood of man, and the
solidarity of the human race is moved exactly in that proportion.
If you could make man live alone he would forget his brother.

With this movement for de-individualization comes this necessary fact ; always, everywhere—there is no exception to it, the world does not present an exception in any prominent sense—capitol, the diffusion of labor, always means the use of tools ; capital—that is a necessary condition—always means production on a large scale. Capital—the thing true, in the large, comprehensive use of capital, is this, that it cheapens products but it does not cneapen products by merely making the same amount cheaper. For example, the shoemaker, if you give him a machine that he may make one hundred pairs of shoes instead of ten pairs, could not do it cheaper, but if he could make a thousand pairs instead of ten, it would be cheaper. Therefore, the large extensive use of product is the first condition of the use of capital. What does that mean ? It means this, that the community must consume in order that the use of capital can be assured.

There is this difference between the attitude of the capitalist to-day and the attitude of the rich man as he was in former periods. The rich man owned everything else, but he did not own capital. The patrician in Rome did not own capital. He scorned the idea of production. What he owned was simply wealth. It was chiefly plunder. It was no economic movement at all. It was not an economic force, but a matter of arbitrary authority. If the rich man to-day could occupy the same position as the baron in the Middle Ages or the patrician of Rome, simply dividing the spoils and plunder, and owning the products of labor by arbitrary authority, then of course his increase in wealth would mean the poverty of the poor. But to-day the rich man does not own the same kind of wealth ; all he owns is productive wealth, and it crumbles unless he uses it advantageously. So that his successful use of his wealth, among other things, necessitates the extensive consumption and diffusion of the simple wealth which he produces. That is somewhat a general principle.

Does it prove to be true in fact ? We often say, " That sounds nice; that is a theory." But now about the facts ? If it is not true in fact, then there is something wrong with the theory and it ought to be rejected. If what I have said is true on general principles we shall find this to follow : wherever the concentration of wealth takes place we shall find that the social individuality of the laborer increases, that his wages rise, that he is elevated, and that the cost of products is lowered. In other words, we shall find these three things, that wealth will be cheapened, that the price of labor will be increased, that moral character and political freedom will be elevated and extended. The facts warrant that conclusion. That is the case. If they do not, then I am out of court.

I do not want to go too far back. The factory system represents the concentration of capital. It moved from hand labor to machine labor within your own memory. The factory represents the system of concentration and economic use of capital. The small water-wheel was, perhaps, the beginning, and the trust the largest form we have yet reached. What have been the marks along the line of that movement? I can see plenty of men and women in this audience who have at one time given twenty cents a yard for cotton cloth. In this country, in 1830, it sold for higher prices than that. At that time there were 801 cotton factories in this country, using a capital of about 40 millions of dollars. They produced an aggregate of 59 millions of pounds of the finished product. In 1880, the number of establishments was reduced, and our population had increased, everything had grown up to 1880 — and in 1880 our cotton manufactories were reduced to 746, with 207 millions of . dollars invested, and a production of 207 millions of pounds of the finished product. How about the laborer? How about the price of cotton cloth and the consumption of cloth? In 1830, the consumption of cotton cloth, per capita, was 6 pounds and 8-10. In 1880, it was 13 and 90-100—more than double. Wages increased by 110 per cent. The price of cotton cloth, during the same period, fell from 17 cents to a little over 5 cents a yard. Who has been robbed in that situation? Who is it that has been plundered, please tell me? The manufacturing concerns have diminished in number, the amount of capital has increased from 40 millions to 607 millions, wages have doubled, the price of cotton cloth has fallen over 60 per cent., and the manufacturer is better off to-day than he was then. Now, I hold, so far as that case is concerned, as representing the factory system in that industry, the community is the absolute gainer.

But how about the operatives? Well, when you talk about the miserable condition of the operatives in those mills as compared with former times, bear in mind that you are not looking at the same people. You have been taught to think of the American ' operative as receiving low wages and a bare subsistence ; but remember that the American laborer is not there ; he has been taking better positions, and the miserable operatives that are painted before you are the lowest of foreign workmen, such as the Hungarians. The condition of the American operatives is in many respects better than it was thirty years ago. Now you will find them among the overseers, members of the middle class; they have elevated right up. Another fact : Take our factory population, and they represent the tag-end of our civilization.   But as compared with other countries, the aggregate is better.   Wages are higher, the average intelligence in the community is better, and the degree of understanding of our institutions, the degree of morality, if you will, the degree of vice, if you will, is improved.   If you give me time I will agree to demonstrate that their moral condition, decided by the degree of crime, decided by the number of arrests among their classes, the number of cases of wife beating and the number of cases of child beating, the number of cases of desertion—take that class of cases and I will agree to demonstrate that the level is actually and absolutely higher than it was thirty years ago ·among our native people.   Unquestionably during the last thirty or forty years wages have risen nearly a hundred per cent.

But the trust ! You say, "is not the purpose of these organizations to raise prices ? " I do not know what the purpose is—they never consulted me in the matter.   I do know this, that they have not raised prices; and I know, next, that they cannot raise prices permanently.   You say, "Has not the Standard Oil Company increased the price of oil ? " and "Has not the sugar trust put up the price of sugar? "   It is true that sugar has increased in price, but that is due to natural causes, the increase in the price of the raw sugars, and in the fact that grocers have decided to have a profit of one-quarter of a cent on a pound for handling it, something that they have never had before.   The members of the sugar trust are shrewd men and they know that if they would put up prices unduly that something would happen.   They are not fools enough to do that.   And it is certain that their profits are not so great now as they were some time ago.   If you think they stand there to get large profits they don't do it.   It is not business, and, in fact, they do not do it.

It is the fashion to talk against the Standard Oil Company, and I understand that it has been said from this platform that that company is responsible for the high price of oil.   That is an entire mistake in examining things.   Nothing is as it seems unless you know how to look at it.   It has taken us hundreds of years to learn that the sun does not rise, and we still speak of it as though it did. Look at this Standard Oil Company first of all when it was in the hands of small men.   I do not know that the trust is the best form of organization, but I stand for this, that the maximum of the concentration of capital is the best way of producing.   That is my opinion. You know that in 1860 oil was worth sixty cents a gallon and that it has fallen in price. But it always fell, in every stage, with the adoption of better methods—remember that. When oil began to be transported in large quantities by means of pipe lines, that was an investment of capital. The Standard Oil Company started in 1880. Remember that oil had dropped from 60 cents a gallon down to about nine cents a gallon by various means. Now, then, there was only nine cents for the whole thing—the cost of crude oil and refining—it was all in the nine cents. You see it has not dropped as much as it did before ; there was not as much chance to drop, if you had taken it all. Let me illustrate. Here is a sponge full of water. A child may take it and squeeze out a large amount of water, but after the child is through with it a strong man could squeeze out very little water. It takes a great economy when the price is squeezed out of the oil to reduce the price still further. The Standard Oil Company took it when it was nearly dry, and in its saving in the manufacture of cans, and in other economies, reduced the price two cents to the community. " They make something ? " Of course they do. They give two cents a gallon to the community, and still have more left than the others who cannot give us anything. Who got the most in that operation ?

How does it get its profit ? It gets it by making another draft on nature. It gets it by its concentration of capital ; it gets it by its economies in production. And it can get it in no other way. Large corporations, large concerns involve necessarily high moral character as a part of their capital in business. They cannot afford to have a community lose faith in their integrity. Profits are never derived from high prices, but always from reducing them. The virtue of the capitalist, the supreme work that he does, is not in robbing his neighbor, but in making another draft on nature, and that is exactly what social progress involves. We cannot get rich by living upon our neighbor ; but we can by knowing how to make nature do more of the work, and hand down more to the community.

There is much said about the Western Union Telegraph Company ; but it is true that the cost of the messages is trifling compared with what it was before that company took hold of it, and various lines were consolidated. And those who advocate government possession of the telegraph lines, will learn by studying the facts, that in England, where the government owns and controls them, they are run at an actual loss of two cents per message which it made up by taxation.

There is not a line of industry in this country where large capital has been concentrated, where three things have not taken place:
prices have been reduced, wages have been increased, and the freedom of the laborer has been extended. And we want impersonal
corporations, because they can be criticised freely, without fear.
And as to the freedom of the laborer, that may be represented by
a comparison of Southern England where the laborer is familiar
with the employer, receives low wages, and must lift his hat to his
superior ; with the North of England, where, under impersonal corporations, wages are much higher, and the laborer much more independent.

TRUSTS.

THE GLADDEN-GUNTON DEBATE.

Dr. GLADDEN.

[From the Chautauqua Assembly Herald, Tuesday, August 27.]

Dr. Gladden said : This is not to be a combat in any sense of
the word, but simply an inquiry after truth. If my friend, Mr.
Gunton, can tell more truth in half an hour than I can, he shall
have my applause. The object of the discussion is simply to find
out what is the truth. My friend spent considerable of his time the
other day in proving that combination in industry and the centralization of capital was a good thing. I think there cannot be any
disagreement between us on that score. I tried to prove that the
factory system is a good thing on the whole; that its effects in
cheapening commodities and reducing prices have been most benefi-
cent ; and that it has also certain intellectual and moral advantages. But I tried to show you also that there were certain disad-
vantages, certain evils, certain drawbacks connected with it that
we must note and try to guard against. It seems to me, that while
the new system is a good thing in that it cultivates interdependence,

it also is tending to eliminate independence, which I think, also, is a good thing. I know from my own constant acquaintance with the laboring classes, of the evil effects of this massing of labor by the great corporations, and I think we ought to perceive those evil effects and guard against them. I believe that corporations are a good thing, but I tried to show that with the good they do, a great deal of evil is done.

I believe it is true, as a matter of fact, that the Trusts have, and are, suppressing wholesome competition. I believe that it is the hope of the Trusts to suppress all competition as far as possible. Have they not, practically, in a good many branches of business suppressed competition almost altogether.

The Standard Oil Company claims to control about seventy-five per cent. of the oil of the country. I think that the figures will show that it does control ninety per cent. Is it wise to put the control of such business as that into the hands of a secret company of men, whose business we know nothing about, men who never show their books, and who are the absolute masters of the whole field ? It seems to me a very dangerous business ; and that we are bound to be on our guard against this danger.

Now, we are told that the trusts have done a great deal toward · cheapening the commodities in which they deal. I think there is a good deal of exaggeration in that statement. I have in my hands — it is, unfortunately, the only document which I can lay my hands upon, which has any figures about it --a pamphlet published by the Standard Oil Company, presenting their own view, and giving their figures, and the table upon the first page, compiled by themselves, shows that while, during the first few years of the oil industry, from 1861 to 1872, when competition was free—it shows that while the annual reduction in the price of oil was 10 per cent.—that is to say, every year the oil was 10 per cent. lower than the previous year during that period, when a sort of combination was formed in 1872, the reduction in the price of oil was about 7 per cent. per annum for the next nine years. In 1881 the Standard Oil Company was formed, and since that time the reduction in the price of refined oil has been at the rate of about two per cent. per annum, in the price of refined oil. And that reduction in price is due to the reduction in the price of crude oil, during that period, for which the Standard Oil Company is not responsible at all. And, in the meantime, the cost of producing the crude oil has steadily increased, owing to the difficulty in boring wells ; while the cost in refining and transportation has steadily decreased, owing to a good many inventions, which the Standard Oil Company has since that time monopolized. Therefore, the price of the refined oil ought to have decreased at a more rapid rate than the price of the crude. But it has not done so ; the decrease in the price of the crude oil has been the more rapid.

Let me give you some figures given By Mr. Dodd, who is the attorney for the Standard Oil Company. Mr. Dodd shows us that in 1875 crude oil was 9 cents and 43-100ths a gallon. In 1887 it was one cent and fifty-nine one-hundredths, so that the reduction in the price of crude oil was 8 and 41-100. At the beginning of that period, refined oil was 25 and 59-100 per gallon ; therefore, if the same reduction had been made in the price of refined, and the price of crude, it would now be 15 and 75-100 per gallon. But the fact is, the price of refined oil now is 6 and 72-100 per gallon. Therefore, he says, you see we have made gradually more reduction in the price of refined oil than in the price of the crude. Now that is standard arithmetic. [Laughter.]

I do not know whether he understands it or not. He seems to think, to understand, that proportion is a matter of subtraction and not of division. The reduction in the price of crude oil has been 83 per cent. ; if the reduction in the price of the refined had been 83 per cent., it would be 4 and 1-100. That would be the right proportion. If the price of refined oil had been reduced in the same proportion as the price of crude oil, it would, instead of 6 and 72-100 per gallon, now be 4 and 1-100 per gallon, a difference of 2 and 71-100 per gallon in favor of the Standard Oil Company. Instead of giving the people one hundred millions of dollars, as they claim, it has taken twenty-seven millions of dollars more than it is entitled to by the very rule of proportion which ought to apply in this case. If the Standard Oil Company had reduced the price of refined oil as much as it did the price of crude oil, we should have twenty-seven millions of dollars now in our pockets which is in the possession of the Standard Oil Company. That is the simple fact.

We can understand something about the purposes of these companies when we understand something of the way in which they have capitalized these companies. We know this, that when a trust is formed, the capital of the trust is very greatly increased over the capital of the companies that entered into the trust. I believe that is the universal history of all trusts. [Applause.]

MR. GUNTON.

Mr. Gunton said : I am not very eloquent, but I will try to be to the point. The doctor commenced by conceding that the

first fifty minutes of my speech Saturday was about right ; that he
agreed substantially with what I said, that the concentration of capital was in the line of progress. It did what I claimed. Therefore,
we have no quarrel. He asks what is the object of the Trust? I
ask what is the effect of Trusts ? Mr. Gladden says that their effect
has been, first, to stop competition. He says, they, of course,
wouldn't stop, if they could help it at a point without the suppres-
sion of competition. And then he proceeds to the blackboard. The
arithmetic does not lie if fairly dealt with, and I want to get at it.
He begins by quoting from a pamphlet published by the Standard
Oil Company as to their effect in reducing the price of oil. I have
got my facts entirely apart from them, and they are just like those.
The reports of the daily commercial journals, such as the daily
Commercial Bulletin and *Journal of Commerce* will give you every
day the market prices. The report of the Chamber of Commerce
contains reports and statistics same as the Produce Exchange, day
to day, month to month, and year to year, and they can be traced
back from the beginning. And there is no need of depending upon
the Standard Oil Company for information.

He says, let us take the Standard Oil Company's pamphlet.
He cited a table early in the pamphlet in which he said that the
price of refined oil had not fallen as much as the price of the crude
oil. He says the real way to test that and how much the Standard
has done is to apply the proportions, taking percentages. Now,
friends, that is the trick of the trade, and the method that the
Doctor there applied—is probably a kind frequently applied, and
probably he intended to apply it properly. But I want to rivet
your attention on the way he puts those facts. He made them lie
like darkness, when they are as true as daylight ; not intention-
ally, but in the use of things to make them do that sort of work.
He says the percentage and the price of crude oil should keep pace
with refined oil—refined oil should keep pace with crude oil.
Now, see here, friends, let us take the percentage on twenty-four and
the percentage on four. You know that twenty per cent. on twenty
or twenty-five on twenty may be a fourth of it—one-fourth is five.
One-fourth of four would be one. Are they alike ? Is one equal
to five ? Is the reduction of five cents in twenty equal to one cent
in four ? The actual reduction is five times as much. It is as dishonest in arithmetic to compare percentages on different bases as it
is to tell straight contrary statements. I have heard people treat
of wages that same way. I remember, not long ago, a man discussing the rise of wages, and he said that wages had risen in Russia as

in America. That is, the same percentage. Yes, let us see how it looks. Russian wages were about 45 cents a day—call it 50 for easy computation. Ten per cent on 50 cents a day is 5 cents a day. In America, we can, to make it easy, call it $2. Ten per cent. on $2 is 20 cents. Ten per. cent. in America means 20 cents, and ten per cent. in Russia means 5 cents. Is there any similarity? Ten per cent. in America means four times as much as in Russia. When you talk about percentages in crude, you must consider the bases upon which your percentages rest, and it is as dishonest as any method ever applied to the public to attempt to call the result of one-fourth of twenty equal to one-fourth of four. Never was the like in the world. What are the facts in the case—the literal actual facts? I will tell you, and to-day's market will tell Mr. Gladden, if he looks. I will risk it this morning. I will take Saturday's closing markets, and this is the fact about crude oil and about refined oil. In 1880— and I am not now relying on Standard Oil figures, but on the article I have prepared, after spending three months investigating the subject, and published in the *Political Science Quarterly*, of which each one of you can have a copy by sending me the postage—in 1880 the price of crude oil was 2.31 cents per gallon, in 1889 (I have brought figures down since the publication of my article) it is 2.45 cts. per gallon; actually .15 cents per gallon dearer to-day than in 1880. Refined oil is two cents less, more than two cents less, than it was in 1880. Now, what becomes of Mr. Gladden's arithmetic? The crude has not fallen at all. It has fallen, but it is up again, and to-day is more than in 1880, and the refined oil is actually two cents lower than in 1880. Now, is there any arithmetic that can be honestly dealt with, either by minister or layman, which can make two equal to nothing or nothing equal to two? I submit it is not so. [Laughter and applause.]

Where does Mr. Gladden's twenty-five millions come from, that the community ought to have? Can you find it out of zero? [Applause and laughter.] Can you find out of two to nothing? Literally, ladies and gentlemen, need any more be said on that point? [Laughter.]

I am reminded that time is short. Let me speak about legitimate competitors. Now, the Standard Oil Company is perhaps the greatest specimen of a monopoly in Mr. Gladden's sense, on this continent. It has had practically no competition since 1880, and some years before practically had no competition. It has had no law to keep it out; but it has kept at the head—as Dr. Paxton said yesterday—by its sheer superiority in supplying the community

9

better and cheaper. That is the reason. That is why it had no competition. Did it raise the price, when, as the Doctor says, it controls nearly 90 per cent? I have shown you how literal facts show you that the price even with the minimum margin, with all competition exhausted, and unable to live, that it has actually reduced the price two cents wholly and absolutely out of its superior methods, with a rising price in raw material. The gates of capital have been open, and if the Standard Oil Company had been foolish enough to keep oil at nine cents, the capital of Europe would have gone in, and the Standard Oil Company would have had to do one of two things—either reduce its price through competition, or buy the other fellows out, which would cost more still. Now, the wisdom of real business men saw this, that the way to keep the field, the way to be unmolested, the way not to have the chances of success undone, was to keep the margin and prices as near cost as possible, so there should be no invitation for new capital to come in and do a cut-throat business. I do not think that it is a benevolent association. I do not believe a word of it. [Laughter.] I do not believe it ever did a thing, so far as oil is concerned, for the benefit of anybody but the Standard Oil Company. But by general laws which govern our social relations, it was to their interest, and they had sense enough to know it, to keep the price down at a small margin, and the result is the price has fallen, even without competition. They have prospered because they have served the community better than the other fellow. " He cannot be hid." [Laughter and applause.]

I would like if I had the time to talk about the man who is thrown out, because he is the man that attracts our sympathies. What becomes of the undersold man? The man in the corner grocery who charges you a third more because he sells so little, and is undersold by Macy, Wanamaker or some other large concern? This is what becomes of him. It will cost the community to keep him at fabulous prices more than it would cost to keep him as a pauper. We could better afford to take every undersold man or concern who charges us 10, 15 or 20 per cent. more because he does so small a business, and pension them than to pay their high prices that their incompetency demands. If we take Dr. Gladden's suggestion, and retain the paupers that they may be equal, as we ought to have retained the hand-loom weaver in order that the competitive factory would be equal, in such a case the result would be offering a premium for incompetency and putting a block in the way of progress. [Applause.]

Dr. Gladden, in a second speech, deprecated the creation of paupers, and the discouragement of individual initiative in business ; insisted upon the fairness of the conclusion drawn from the statistics presented by him in his first speech ; characterized the rebates received from railroad companies by the Standard Oil Company as robbery, and urged in conclusion the promotion of a public opinion that will watch the trusts, and secure a proper supervision of them.

Mr. Gunton, in reply, criticized Dr. Gladden for his persistence in clinging to his interpretation of his statistics; explained the rebate from a business standpoint, characterizing it as one of the most moral principles in business; urged attention to the results of this line of business, and to the facts attainable, and advised a minimum of government.

[From the New York Sun, Aug. 28, '89.]

THE DEBATE AT CHAUTAUQUA.

Mr. Gunton is a clear-headed gentleman, with no superabundance of sentiment and very little training in debate.   Had he possessed more experience, he would have handled the Rev. Washington Gladden much more effectually.   He would not have permitted himself to lose his temper simply because his antagonist was disingenous and untruthful.   It is only a hasty and hot-tempered man who gets really angry because his opponent is a fool or a bully. He should have left Mr. Gladden at entire liberty to state and to reiterate that 4 is 25 per cent. of 20.   Such arguments furnish their own confutation, and the wisest plan to pursue with an orator of the Gladden variety is to give him all the rope he desires and let him hang himself as soon as possible.

We approve greatly of the wholesale discussion of the Trusts that is taking place, although we see clearly that the better they are understood the more numerous they will become, and the more generally they will be participated in.   In England, which is a free-trade country, there is no important industry and few small ones in an untrusted condition.   All classes of people have given in their adherence to the Trust idea, and it has also taken hold of labor with a vengeance.   Combination for protection is the motto of all ranks of people, and the end is not yet visible.

Labor combines. Capital combines. As a general thing capital has so far got a little the start of labor in the struggles between the two. But in the end it will come out all right. Natural law will prevail in the long run, as it has done invariably since the waters receded from this globe. The eternal principle of Demand and Supply will regulate all things, and all the Trusts that the ingenuity of man may devise will not prevail one jot or tittle against it.

And no unjust Trust shall live. The Trust that is oppressive must fall.

If refined oil is put at an unnatural price, the Standard Oil Company will be smashed. Millions of money will be forthcoming to make and sell oil at a legitimate profit, and the Standard will go to the wall. Is sugar too dear? If it be, down goes the Sugar Trust! And we note by the way that the capital has been promptly forthcoming to put up a plant to make a thousand tons of sugar a day in Philadelphia in opposition to this self-same Sugar Trust. The profit of the trust on its output is only a fraction of a cent per ·pound, and yet here are millions of money furnished to wrest that profit from it and divide it among competing manufacturers. Whose liberties are in any real danger under such circumstances as these? Nobody's; unless, indeed, it be that grave danger threatens the capitalists.

And it is so with every Trust from the Standard Oil down to the Peanut, and the inevitable tendency is to anticipate the point at which any injustice is about to be inflicted on the public. A fraction of a cent on sugar has precipitated a powerful competition. A cent a gallon on cotton oil did not imply any grievous hardship on the consumers of the pure lard into which the bulk of cotton oil is converted, or on the consumers of the pure olive oil which is so largely manufactured from it. It was enough, however, to precipitate competition, and the Cotton Oil Trust has to fight for its living just as if it was a grocery fighting another grocery across the way.

Such is the inevitable and the necessary destiny of the Trusts. That it should be otherwise is as impossible as it is inconsistent with the natural law and with the principles of human progress. Hence our contempt for the outcries of demagogues, and the silly clamor to impose artificial and legislative restraints upon the natural expedients of intelligent business men. The Trusts are modern business expedients, and they will exist and undergo their own regulation. It may be safely set down that the attacks that are made on them have their foundation in ignorance or in envy. Mr. Gladden is a very ignorant and harmless assailant, and was not worth the notice accorded to him, but the greater number of those who have attacked the Trust publicly and through the press have had no honest motive in doing so. Some of them have been hypocrites and demagogues by training and habit ; some of them have wanted to blackmail their way into Trusts where they were not wanted ; some of them were in Trusts themselves already, but could not on that account tolerate the Trusts of their neighbors ; and all of them had poor motives, and they will remain to the end convinced that there is nothing so infamous as a Trust that they do not participate in.

[From the AMERICAN ECONOMIST, July 12, 1889.]

THE SUGAR TRUST.

We have no sympathy with any scheme which tends to unduly increase the price of any commodity which is in general use among the people. If it can be shown that the Sugar Trust has used the power of combination to advance the price of sugar unfairly and thereby increase the living expenses of the people of this country we will heartily support measures to suppress it; but we do not unite with the blind mob in howling down any organization or combination until it is shown that it is a wrong.

We have regretted to observe in a leading Republican paper what seems to be an unreasonable assault upon the Sugar Trust. It declares that the price of raw sugar has been advanced from 4.44 cents per pound in 1887 to 7 cents at the present time, and that the refiners now receive 1.94 per pound additional for the granulated and 2.44 cents per pound additional for the crushed, instead of 1.50 cents and 1.68 cents, respectively, two years ago. The article then proceeds to charge upon the Sugar Trust the whole difference between the present price of sugar consumed in the United States and the price two years ago, amounting to $97,-500,000. We do not hesitate to say that this charge is unjust and is more like the mischievous harangues of an irresponsible demagogue than the thoughtful, well-considered reflections of an intelligent, sober, metropolitan editor.

The facts in the case are too well-known to be disguised.   For
a long series of years the foreign price of raw sugar prior to 1884
remained nearly uniform, averaging from 4½ cents to 5 cents per
pound, and the American price, with duty added, averaging from 6½
to 7 cents per pound.   Sometimes, in the course of 25 years, the
average price would go below 6½ cents and sometimes above 7
cents.   In 1872, for example, the average foreign price of raw sugar
was over 5⅜ cents per pound, and with duty added cost in the
United States about 7⅜ cents, or higher than the price to-day,
which is charged to the manipulation of the trust.   Since 1884 the
extraordinary increase in the production of sugar has caused a
rapid decline in price until in 1887 the average cost of raw sugar
landed in the United States, duty paid, was less than 4½ cents per
pound.   The details of this increase and decline are thus stated in
a recent report to the English Board of Trade, published in the
London *Economist* of June 15 :

The increase in the production of sugar, which was noticed as so remarkable in the report of 1884, has been even more remarkable since.   It was stated
in 1884 that in 1853 or thereabouts the total sugar production recorded, according to the circular of Messrs. Rueb & Ledeboer, was only 1,400,000 tons ; in
1878, which was just before the Sugar Bounties Committee in 1879-80, the total
was just over 3,000,000 tons, and in 1882, the last year dealt with in the report
of 1884, it was 3,800,000 tons.   The increase to 1878 was 110 per cent. in 25
years, and in the following years, from 1878 to 1882, the increase was about 26
per cent.   Now it has to be added that since 1882 there has been an increase to
5,500,000 tons in the last complete year, or, making certain corrections, to 5,200,-
000 tons, the amount being now nearly four times the total in 1853, when the
statistics begin.

The increase in production has been in all descriptions of sugar, but prin-
cipally in beet-sugar, which, from being an inconsiderable part of the total
production, has come to be nearly equal in importance to cane.   While in 1853
the production was over 1,200,000 tons cane to rather less than 200,000 tons
beet, the production of beet on the average of 1886-87 was 2,430,000 tons out of an
average total of nearly 5,200,000 tons, while the production of cane was 2,750,-
000 tons.   The production of beet has thus increased about 12 times, while
cane-sugar has little more than doubled, the result being that the two sources of
supply are now nearly level with each other.

In 1884 it was noted that the fall in sugar at that time was not greater than
in the case of other staple articles, such as teas, wheat, cotton, wool, etc.   Since
1884 there is no doubt there has been a special decline in sugar.   In 1884 the
decline in refined sugar from the 1861 standard was about 17¼ per cent. and in
raw sugar 9¼ per cent., the decline in the other articles referred to ranging from
about 15 to 38 per cent. ; but refined sugar now shows a decline of about 55 per
cent. from the 1861 standard and raw sugar 48 per cent., while the decline in
other articles ranges from 27 to 42 per cent. only.

The effect of this remarkable decline in price was shown especially in a rapidly increasing *per capita* consumption, so that at the close of the year 1887 there had been no material increase of the supply. A further effect growing out of a diminished supply in Cuba and the East is seen in a sudden and rapid return of the world price to the level which prevailed before the decline began. The report to which we have already referred notes an advance in the London price of raw sugar from under 14s. per cwt. in the beginning of 1889 to 22s. on the 24th of May, or more than 60 per, cent. Since then a further advance has taken place.

With this evidence of the general advance all over the world, and no greater in proportion here than elsewhere, how is it possible to charge it upon the operations of the American Sugar Trust? The only advance which can with any reason be charged upon the Trust is the increase of the difference above stated between the price of raw and refined—44-100 cent on the granulated and 50-100 cent on the crushed, say half a cent per pound, or 25 cents per annum per head of our population, assuming that they all use only the refined sugar.

Whether this advance is reasonable is an open question. It is well known that the business of sugar-refining was, for many years prior to the organization of the Trust, disastrous. Competition among the parties engaged in it resulted in loss, and combination to protect themselves and those in their employ would seem to be not only legitimate, but for the advantage of the community. For it is not desirable that any important industry should perish for want of adequate means of securing reasonable profits, and the community is as much interested as individuals in seeing such means adopted precisely as towns remit taxes, or give bonds to induce the establishment of an important industry. At any rate, an advance of one-half a cent in the price paid the refiners for their work can hardly be made the ground for the charge of extortion, when it is known that at the old rates their business was going on at a loss.

The worst aspect of the assault on the Sugar Trust, and its unfounded charges, is its effect upon what promises to become one of our great national industries—the production of raw sugar. It has been known by German experience that it is possible for this nation to become independent of all other nations for its supply of sugar. Germany, with no better, if as good, advantages than we have in the United States, has within a few years become an exporter instead of an importer of sugar. In fact, her production has been the prime factor which has reduced the price of sugar for all civilized nations. Although a return to old prices has now occurred, no one familiar with the facts will deny that the advance will be of short duration. A falling off in consumption, together with increase of production, following high prices, will speedily bring back the conditions of last year, with every prospect of permanency.

It is especially important at this critical period of the American sugar industry, that no unjust prejudices should be excited, and that all who desire the establishment of a great industry among us, with its immense results for the general welfare of our people, should unite in forming a fair and just public opinion upon all branches of this sugar question. It affects our whole people, as almost no other question affects them, and they may be easily misled by unfair and unconsidered statements into a public policy which will in the future prove an incalculable injury.

The stocks of sugar in the chief European markets, May 1, 1889, were 604,000 tons, against 743,000 a year ago. This is a decline of nearly 20 per cent. On the other hand, the consumption of sugar in Europe for the year ending May 1, 1889, was 2,818,000 tons, against 2,657,000 tons the previous year. In other words, we find an increase of 20 per cent. in the consumption within one year. It is noted also that the stocks of sugar in England and the United States were at the same time 200,000 tons less than they were a year ago. Besides this, Licht, the highest authority on the subject, reports the world's visible supply at 735,000 tons, against upward of a million a year ago.

The consumption of sugar in the United States increased remarkably with the decline in price during the past ten years. In 1877-'78 when the price of raw sugar was 7¼ to 7½, the consumption was 36 pounds *per capita.* In 1882-'83 it increased to 45 pounds and in 1888 it was 53 pounds. We have here an increase of nearly 50 per cent. in the consumption of the United States *per capita* in ten years, owing chiefly to the decline in price.

Are not these facts ample to explain the rise in raw sugar without calling in the bugbear of the Sugar Trust and exciting popular prejudice against the continuance of Protection for American sugar interests.

[From THE CHRISTIAN ADVOCATE, August 22, 1889.]

TRUSTS.

By JAMES McGEE.

[Paper read before Religious Press Club April 9, Methodist Ministers May 20, Society of Christian Philosophy June 6, 1889.]

The word trust is one of the most sacred in the English language ; whether we employ it in its verb form, denoting confidence imposed, or its substantive form, implying accepted responsibility, there is that which appeals to the intelligent mind as conveying the thought of security.

There is, nevertheless, an apparent effort to deprive the community of its use, or so to limit the application as to make void the confidence which, on the one side, has been imposed, and on the other accepted.

In this effort portions of the secular and religious press have joined. Magazines and journals discussing the question from a professedly economic standpoint have arrayed themselves on the one side or the other according to their theories of economic science. Some portions of the religious press have sought to charge the commercial or business features of trusts with principles opposed to morality, and still further to invest the very form of a trust with all the odious features of a conspiracy against public interest and a complete violation of the decalogue and the Sermon on the Mount.

Against the false theories of political economists and the unchristian torture of religious formulas it is no less the duty than the right of those who have given or accepted these trusts to protest.

In attempting the further discussion of this question, if it is to be at all profitable, three principles must be kept in mind : first, there must be a frank recognition of evils actual or possible ; second, there must be a fair consideration of arguments pro and con ; third, there must be a sincere effort to reach conclusions which on the one hand shall not fetter trade nor, on the other, impose burdens on society.

Before proceeding more directly on these lines of thought let us clear the way by some statements which will bring us up to the question at issue.

CLEARING THE WAY.

First of all, let us observe that necessity is laid on commerce to find new forms of business to meet the new conditions with which it is confronted. Three great factors have been introduced into the commercial world in a comparatively short period of time —the railroad, the steamship and the telegraph. Those who are old enough to remember the methods of business previous to the introduction of these elements will not have failed to notice the changes that have been introduced. Many doubtless regret these changes, but society at large has reaped the benefit. The railroad has opened up vast tracts of country and made it possible to occupy and subdue them. The steam-ship has furnished facilities for rapidly transferring the productions of the earth from one quarter of the globe to another. The land and ocean wires have so covered all sections of the world with their net-work that, as if part of a great nervous system, each responds instantaneously to the other.

It is now possible for a merchant in India to cable an order for a cargo of merchandise to his correspondent in New York, who, receiving it on 'change, buys the merchandise, engages the freight, sells the exchange, and cables back the execution of the order, the whole being done sometimes within a few hours.

This state of affairs has led to the introduction of many new methods of business, some of which may be of doubtful value. Among these may be noted the multiplication of exchanges, the wider application of the " call-room," the introduction of "rings " for the rapid execution of orders, the much larger dealing in " futures," new methods of inspection and classification of goods, systems of statistical information bringing the wants and facilities of the world before the business man not only daily but hourly, and, so far as market reports are concerned between places depending on each other, even momentarily.

It will be needless to say that all this has made competition keen and capital eager. What more natural under these circumstances than that new forms of business should be devised? The law which controls the concentration of capital is as uniform in its application as the law of supply and demand. Wherever a new mine is discovered there capital enters at once, eager to invest in its claims or to supply the needs of those engaged in developing them. So, too, in all articles of production and manufacture the tendency is to concentrate capital, reduce cost of production, and make the bridge between the producer and consumer as short as possible. This may be aptly illustrated by the proposal which was seriously made to do in one company all that is involved in the meat business, from the raising of the cattle to the delivery to the consumer.

The natural consequence of this state of affairs is an overproduction in all departments of growth and manufacture, resulting in many commercial disasters. At this point the community looks on and seems careless of results, thinking that it benefits by the unwise competition and does not suffer by the disaster. No argument is needed to refute this selfish view. When, however, some attempt is made to avoid the evils of overproduction, and give some stability to business, then a great hue and cry is raised by the same public who looked on with complacency at the results of extreme competition and overproduction.

Let us look now at the organization of a trust. A number of persons finding themselves owners in common of the stock of several companies engaged in one line of business, and believing that these companies can be run more economically and efficiently if brought into closer relationship, agree to place their stock in the hands of trustees, who shall in turn issue certificates showing the amount of interest of each owner in the stock so held in trust. Now what is sought to be accomplished ? I will answer in the words of the distinguished counsel who gave form to the first of the trusts, properly so called :

The stockholders thereby become interested in all the corporations whose stock is thus held. The trustees elect the directors of the several corporations. The different corporations preserve their autonomy, but the result undoubtedly intended and reached is that the corporations become co-operative rather than competitive—that is, they are not competitive in the sense of trying to injure and destroy each other, but are competitors in the better sense of each trying to do the best and most effective work at the least cost, and to show the best results. They are co-operative in the sense of each being able to obtain the benefit of any knowledge, experience, or improvement known to the other.

Let me add here an extract from an editorial notice in a commercial paper, of high standing, which has bitterly opposed trusts. Speaking of the American Meat Company, before referred to, which, though not a trust, proposed to do, by a large capital and a combination of various interests, all that can be done by any trust, it says:

Having secured all these advantages the company naturally expects to eliminate the profits of the middlemen, to secure the economy resulting both

from concentrated management and from an ability to purchase material in
large quantities, and at low cost, and to have at all times a certain and profitable
outlet for its productions.

Here is clearly an intention and expectation to accomplish ob-
jects so often put down to the discredit of trusts ; namely, middlemen are to be eliminated, management concentrated, purchases to
be made at lowest cost, and thus a certain and profitable outlet for
its productions secured.   The result is certainly commendable, and
is spoken of without disapproval, and this is just what is proposed
by a trust.

INDICTMENT OF TRUSTS BY THEIR OPPONENTS.

We will allow the opponents of trusts, however, to make their
own indictment, which we understand to be substantially as follows:
First. "Trusts" make possible such concentration of capital as that
a comparatively few rich men may control the commerce of the
world.   Second. They present inducements to the use of unlawful
means to accomplish the end proposed.   Third. Having secured by
any means the control of an article or articles of commerce the result is used to force exactions from society.

A general answer to this indictment, and it would appear a sufficient one, is that none of the things complained of originated with,
nor are they a natural product of, that form of business known as
a "trust."   We will seek, however, to make more specific answer.

The first charge is essentially that of monopoly, not granted
by the Government, but practically secured by the concentration of
capital.   Fortunately the Government of this country does not and
cannot grant a monopoly, nor can the concentration of capital secure it.   It is supreme folly in this age to suppose that any amount
of capital which has been invested in a commercial enterprise cannot be duplicated.   Let the conditions justify, and the work will be
done.   As sure as the filings will follow the magnet so sure will capital feel the attraction of commercial profit.   When a great railroad
was supposed to be making money too fast it was readily paralleled.
The business represented in the first trust has very successful competitors.   When a later trust was started a merchant single-handed
entered the arena and prepared to wrestle with the problem and secure a return for his investment.   The cry of monopoly is the wail
of disappointment.   One has well said that the strongest opponents
of monopoly are those who would be monopolists.   The world may
be safely·challenged to show such a control of any article of merchandise (except under a government monopoly) as would prevent
others from successfully competing.

Others, however, allege that if a monopoly is not really obtained, still competition is practically defeated.   This word competition seems to be the sole economic law known to many people.   Their motto is "competition is the life of trade;" in reality, however, competition is often the destruction of trade.

Self-preservation is a law of business as well as of nature. The means of self-preservation in business, however, are not necessarily confined to competition.   Take the smallest trader in a country town; he is prosperous, the community grows and he grows with it in prosperity.   He is not exacting, but content with fair profits. An envious eye rests on his prosperity.   A competitor enters the field and reduces the profits.   This is met with further reduction by the older dealer.   The community are pleased; competition has served their ends.   By and by both dealers fail, and some one else pays for the competition.   Would it have been a sin for these parties to have combined their forces, shared the business, divided the profits, main-tained their credit, and saved those trusting them from loss?

After writing this theoretical case a daily paper furnished the practical illustration in an incident headed " Two Foolish Butchers," and which is as follows :

A butchers' war has excited New Brunswick and at the same time amused it. The whole place is taking advantage of the cut in prices caused by the war, and yet there seems to be no sign of its abatement. The rivalry is between two butchers owning opposite stands on Burnet street, one of the principal streets in the city. One of them made a reduction in prices, and the other cut under. Further reductions followed until meats are selling for half price. Some kinds, indeed, are selling for less. One of the butchers finally offered some of his meats for sale at four cents a pound. The other offered the same kind at three cents and agreed to throw in a head of cabbage with each pur-chase. One of them had his store front completely covered with American flags, to attract attention, whereupon the other engaged a brass band, which he says will play in his shop to draw trade. Both butchers are losing money heav-ily, while all the others are losing trade, but neither shows any sign of giving up the fight.

Another journal, commenting on this incident asks, " Why fool-ish ? " when the very paper which contained the incident was in an-other column opposing " trusts," the object of which is to prevent this same foolishness on a much larger scale.

This fear of combination is an old one, but generally without reason.   It had its day in England, and enacted stupid laws which were subsequently repealed.   Professor Dwight, in *Political Science Quarterly*, December, 1888, says of these repealed acts, " They tes-tify to the ignorance of Parliament, the puerility of judges, the subservience of juries, and the sufferings of their victims, but little more." A committee of the House of Commons reported that these laws had been the means of accomplishing the very object they were intended to prevent, namely, of raising the price of commodities. The operation is simple. Restrict and hamper trade, make it unlawful to combine capital and other resources, and immediately society goes back to first principles. The few who have the means provide only for their own wants or so much more as they can get large profits for. Society, instead of being served by the restriction, is itself restricted in supplying its own wants.

That competition is not always healthy has come to be recognized by the courts of this country, and in some cases it has been specifically so set forth. The law of competition then, is this—the channels of trade must be free to all. The return of capital, while proportioned to the risks assumed, must not be exorbitant. These principles no trust or combination can violate without risking its commercial existence. There is nothing in the form of a trust which makes easier the violation of these principles than is found in any corporate existence.

The second count in the indictment is the charge of using unlawful means to secure financial success. This charge is very vague except in one thing, and that is, the giving and receiving large rebates on railroad freights. A favorite method of stating this problem is to take the highest so-called "open rate," deduct the lowest "cut rate," and, using the difference for a multiplier, calculate the amount on all the goods of a particular kind to which it is applicable and declare that this amount has gone into the pockets of the shipper. This is very far, however, from the true state of the case. The rebate system was the fovorite law of competition at work, only in this case among the railroads, and the community reaped the benefit in a very large measure. Up to the time of the appointment of the Interstate Commerce Commission the rebate was the rule, not the exception. The rates were flexible, each shipper made his own bargain, and in not a few cases the smaller shipper had the larger rebate. The public were well satisfied to take their share of the rebate. Their indignation was only aroused when any part was supposed to find its way into the pocket of the shipper. Rebates are now abolished by law. Severe penalties are inflicted upon any who give or receive them, and therefore this issue can no longer be used as an argument against trusts. The system did not originate with, nor is it necessary to the continuance of, any trust.

The third count in the indictment is that, a practical monopoly being secured, it is used to make heavy exactions upon society. Speaking for one, and that one the first in order of the trusts, the facts do not warrant this conclusion.

If we go back to 1880 we find the price of crude petroleum to average about ninety-four cents per barrel, with refined oil averaging about nine cents per gallon, while this year, when crude was ranging at about the same price, refined oil was selling at about seven cents per gallon. Not only are the facts against the conclusion, but the laws of trade will render of short duration any attempt to maintain prices above a fair level. The laws of competition, supply and demand, and conservative banking enter into the problem and the bubble bursts. A commercial journal already quoted as bitterly opposed to trusts, in a valuable article on the collapse of the copper syndicate, has stated the law in terse language. "An advance in price stimulates production and decreases consumption ; the more artificial the advance the more rapid the effect."

If there was a fair chance for any syndicate to make artificial prices it was the copper syndicate. Backed by almost fabulous foreign capital, it sought to control the markets of the world, and signally failed, wrecking the Societe des Meteaux, and the Comptoir De Escompte. If then the *facts* and the *laws of trade* do not sustain this third count of the indictment it will readily be seen that *business policy* will suggest a careful adherence to those principles which alone can insure perpetuity.

There are other abjections urged, however, which, not being stated in as logical a form, are the better calculated to mislead.

Attention is frequently called to the fact that by the combination of several companies factories are closed, owners are paid without rendering service, while workmen are left without employment and consequently to suffer.

In making these statements, however, it is very carefully concealed from view that from the lack of agreement or concert of action—that is, under the untrammeled sway of competition—numerous factories have been closed, owners wrecked, and employes disbanded, and in this way probably twice the harm has been done that can be laid at the door of any combination.

Again, it is very much descanted upon that these combinations are not formed for philanthropic purposes, and consequently avail themselves of every opportunity to prey upon the community. Now, let it be distinctly understood that it is not claimed that business operations are set on foot from purely philanthropic motives, but

it is claimed that the love of adventure and the desire of gain which
is prominent in all commercial transactions, large or small, can
through these larger channels be made subservient to the public
good by bringing to the door of the consumer at the lowest possible
cost the articles needed for his daily use.

We have lately been treated to figures in the daily press showing the cost to the people of a single one-tenth of a cent per pound
on any one of the great articles of consumption.

The figures doubtless are correct, but they are intended to de-
ceive; the other side is thoughtfully suggested by Erastus Wiman,
Esq., in a brochure entitled "The Waste of Competition." He
asks "What money has ever been made in handling sugar, the world
over, till in the last few months? How many team leads of sugar
have been handled up hill and down dale without a cent of profit?
How many thousands of millions of pounds have been weighed and
papered and twined by hundreds of thousands without a cent—a
solitary cent—of profit?" And as a final question asks, what we do
well to ponder, "Who is the better off for all this sacrifice?"

Incidental conditions of business are often made use of as illustrations of the tendency of "Trusts." Thus, for example, it is
charged that certain corporations, notably gas companies, which
have had a quasi monopoly, have uniformly maintained high prices.
This, if true now, was true before "Trusts" had an existence, and
therefore cannot be chargeable to them. The difficulty doubtless
was and is a lack of local facilities or of local enterprise.

A final objection which I shall answer is one which is made
not only against " Trusts," but against the increase and development of all corporations. At once the most popular and the most
tangible of all objections, if seriously considered, it carries with it
its own answer. It is stated thus : In the advance and extension
of corporations the individual is being organized out of society. The
difficulty is to know just what is meant; but if it means any thing it
must be that a few people are being lifted up above the masses,
while the masses themselves are either making no advance or are
retrograding—but in what direction ? It must be in morals, intellect, social equality or ability to live. Now as to morals; bad as
many things still are, yet who does not remember a time, not far
in the past, when many things which would not now be tolerated
were unblushingly exhibited. And has not Christianity in its organized form taken a greater hold on the masses? Dr. Dorchester, in
Problem of Religious Progress, page 457, states the evangelical population in 1800 to have been 24 per cent. of the whole, while in 1880

it was 70 per cent. Turn now to the intellectual development, and let the Chautauqua Scientific Circle answer, penetrating farm-house and factory; hovel and cottage. Let the hundreds of thousands of magazines and religious and secular newspapers answer.

Now as to social status, let James Brice, in the *American Commonwealth*, answer. Comparing European countries with the United States, he says :

Contrast any of these countries with the United States, where the working-classes are well fed, clothed, and lodged as the lower middle class in Europe, and the farmers who till their own land (as nearly all do) much better, where a good education is within the reach of the poorest, where the opportunities for getting on in one way or another are so abundant that no one need fear any physical ill but disease or the results of his own intemperance. Pauperism already exists and increases in some of the larger cities, where drink breeds misery, and where recent immigrants, with the shiftlessness of Europe still clinging around them, are huddled together in squalor. But outside these few cities one sees nothing but comfort. In Connecticut and Massachusetts the operatives in many a manufacturing town lead a life far easier, far more brightened by intellectual culture and amusements than that of the clerks and shop-keepers of England or France. In cities like Cleveland or Chicago one finds miles on miles of suburb filled with neat wooden houses, each with its tiny garden plot, owned by the shop assistants and handicraftmen who return on the horse cars in the evening from their work. All over the wide West, from Lake Ontario to Upper Missouri, one travels past farms of two to three hundred acres, in every one of which there is a spacious farm-house among orchards and meadows, where the farmer's children grow up strong and hearty on abundant food, the boys full of intelligence and enterprise, ready to push their way on farms of their own or enter business in the nearest town; the girls familiar with the current literature of England as well of America.

Once more, look at the ability to live, the touch-stone of so many political economists.

Bradstreet's of May 18, 1889, commenting on some figures furnished by the *Chicago Inter-Ocean*, comparing prices of one hundred years ago with to-day, says:

With these comparisons in mind it becomes significant to read that the average price of day-labor at the date referred to was fifty cents. We may admit that the corresponding wages to-day are $1.50, which points to the payment for services having *increased* nearly three times within the century, while many of the real necessities of life have *decreased* in price in a corresponding or still greater ratio.

Now, where has the individual been organized out of society? Perhaps it may be said in lack of personal independence ; but may we not ask, How can a decline of personal independence be consistent with an advance in morals, intellect, social status, and ability to live ?

10

Having thus answered the objections as far as they have been formulated, I remark that it may be true there is now a tendency to overdo "Trusts," that many have not been well considered, that some will disappear, and, if so, then the principles already indicated will have worked out their natural results.

It may be safely affimed that no "Trust" will stand the test of time that does not bend it energies in combining all its experience and skill to the end that the community may reap the advantages in cheap and good articles of commerce, reserving only for itself a fair profit for the risks assumed. These are the principles that must govern the individual merchant, co-partnership, joint stock or limited liability corporation. Nor is there any thing in the form of a trust that gives it any advantage over either of these, if the same capital and experience are joined in them.

WHY THE PLAN OF "TRUSTS" IS ADOPTED.

It may then probably be asked, Why adopt this plan? In answering we note, first, negatively, it is not for the purpose of assuming corporate powers without their responsibility. The trustees do not transact the business of the corporation whose stocks are held in trust. Their work is to receive, care for and divide to the shareholders the funds coming into their hands. They may be, and in most instances are, directors of some of the allied corporations, and thus give to them the benefit of their experience and counsel; but this they would do if the companies were not joined in a trust. Professor Dwight says:

It is not a nuisance at common law for persons, no matter how many, to agree to form an unincorporated association and to issue certificates of shares representing property contributed, nor to make the certificates transferable either by written assignment or by delivery, nor to establish a committee having power to make rules for the government of the association. Persons doing these acts do not usurp the functions of a corporation, for the great and distinguishing feature of a corporation is the possession of such juristic qualities as to be a new legal person, distinct from the individuals forming it. To usurp the functions of a corporation there must be the usurpation of the qualities of a "person," as, for example, to sue or to be sued in an assumed corporate name.

It is not for the purpose of evading taxation. The several companies are organized under the laws of the States where they exist, and are subject to taxation according to those laws.

It is not for the purpose of a spasmodic raid on markets; this may be the work of corners, not of trusts.

It has been well said that "a distinct line should be drawn between 'corners' and manufacturing and distributing enterprises, although 'corners' usually re-act upon their promoters."

Coming, then, to the positive side, they are organized :

First. Because it is an easy and effective method of combining the capital, experience, and resources of companies operating in different States.

Second. Because only in such combinations can the lowest cost of production and distribution be secured.

Third. Because, the laws of the several States differing so widely in their provisions, a trust seems to present the only method by which business can be conducted throughout the Union.

The American Grocer, a journal which has very guardedly reached its conclusions on the subject of trusts, says, " There must be organizations of trade as well as of labor, and the only standard by which they can be judged is the reasonableness of their actions. If they are unreasonable they can be indicted under the common law ·for conspiracy and punished, but reasonable action to avoid unreasonable competition should not be condemned ; and it is safe to say that as soon as the economic facts become apparent they will not be." What, then, is the contention of this paper ? That there are no dangers to be feared from the concentration of capital and no difficulties to be overcome in seeking to avert these danger s? Certainly not.

This is the contention : that capital must and will concentrate, and that the form of a trust, so far from menacing the welfare of a community, is likely to give economy and stability to business from which society will reap great advantages.

Is it not reasonable that those who oppose " trusts " should give some definite view as to what is proposed in their destruction ?

So far as these views are exhibited they are as spectral as the " specter in the market " which they have conjured up as the form of "trusts." We can, however, see through their specter sufficiently to determine what gives it form.

First. Opposition to growth of individual wealth; this is communism. Remember that when the process of division begins it only ends with a complete overthrow of individual right in property. Are we prepared for this ?

Second. A higher form of socialism, which, admitting the advantages of " trusts," would "have all industries operated in the interests of all by the nation." This is the creed of the National Club of Boston. Are we prepared for this ?

Third. Opposition to the aggregation of corporate wealth. This means that the nineteenth century has witnessed the maximum power that can be profitably employed by corporations. Is it possible that with the vast work yet to be done in the world there is to be no advance along the line of business methods? If so, many enterprises must be left unaccomplished until broader views prevail.

Fourth. But the real background of the specter is our old friend Competition. Is it not pertinent to ask why those who have such an admiration for competition on a small scale stand aghast when it is proposed on a larger scale? " Trusts" represent competition on a higher plane. The New York State Senate Committee say "combination grows out of and is a natural development of competition, and in many cases it is the only means left to the competitors to escape absolute ruin."

Would it not be well, before seeking by legislative enactment to destroy "trusts," to note the words of warning uttered by the same Committee when they say :

It should, however, be borne in mind that the trust is not indigenous to this age or country only ; that in one form or another it has existed in every prosperous commercial community from the most remote and primitive ages in every part of the world, and among every people of whose social institutions we have any information. It would seem reasonable to conclude that phenomena of such wide development in the world of trade must be the result of natural law, which, while it might be advantageous to the people to subject to reasonable artificial restraint, still exists, like all natural law, for some useful purpose, and that its total destruction, even if such a result could be brought about by laws of our own making, a fact which is extremely doubtful, instead of contributing to the public welfare would be the greatest of public calamities.

ABUSES TO BE CORRECTED.

That there are many abuses to be corrected cannot be denied. These abuses, however, are the outgrowth of selfishness and avarice, which may be manifested in any form of business. The world is growing better, not worse. Careful legislation may overcome many of the evils, but not by giving to one class the privilege of combining and denying it to the other, nor by such crude legislation as is now proposed in several States. In one State it is proposed to make it a misdemeanor punishable by fine or imprisonment, or both, for two or more persons to combine *capital, skill or acts* to *increase* or *reduce* the price of merchandise or commodities; and another act, actually passed, makes it a misdemeanor to sell any class of goods, raw or manufactured, *for less than actual cost* for the purpose of breaking down competition. Now what is this latter but a combination to maintain prices at certain fixed rates, as high, at least, as cost, we thus defeating the very law of competition which the act is passed to sustain?

It may be the time has come for the General Government to

take another step in the line of the Interstate Commerce act, and give charters to companies doing business in the several States. The following extract from *Popular Science Monthly* may serve to indicate a drift of public opinion :

> For trusts limiting their operations to the United States a line of treatment has been suggested which has doubtless had its origin in legal consideration of the railroad question. Since its settlement is stoutly maintained by expert authority to consist in frank acceptance of the pool and its legalization, why not, it is asked, also legalize the trust, surrounding its control with all the safeguards necessary and feasible? The State already exercises a degree of supervision over certain quasi public business—banking, insurance, and railroading. Its supervision may be justly extended to the trusts, while at the same time the levy of a just tax will make the people sharers in the advantages of trust organizations.

Whatever the evils, however they are to be corrected, the work will not be done by calling names or heaping up abuse.

There are mighty enterprises to be accomplished and immense aggregations of capital will be required to do the work. We read of ships bringing away the laborers from the Panama Canal, and we are told that $50,000,000 would finish the work. The time may not be far distant when there shall be one hundred men who will be ready to place a million each in some trust that will finish a highway between the two great oceans.

Is it too much to suppose that commerce will have a share in the literal fulfillment of ancient prophecy, " Every valley shall be exalted, and every mountain and hill shall be made low ? "

Two things are needed for the reconciliation of capital and labor and the allaying of fears on either side : There must be a broad and comprehensive provision for the commerce of the world, and there must be an equally broad and comprehensive recognition of the responsibility imposed by wealth. This done, capital and labor, guarded alike by righteous laws, shall go hand in hand, harvesting and distributing, equitably and economically, the resources of the earth.

[From THE (N. Y.) STANDARD.]

MEN AND THINGS.

When an engineer designs an arch, an important factor in his calculations is the thrust—the tendency of the arch to push its sup-porting piers apart. The great copper syndicate sought to build an arch whose supports were demand and supply. They made no allowance for the thrust. So soon as they laid upon their arch the load that they intended it to bear, the supporting piers separated, and the arch tumbled into ruin.

There are in the world a certain number of deposits of copper, from which human labor can produce the metal with varying advantages. For purposes of comparison, these deposits, or mines, may be represented by a series of figures beginning, say, with four, and ending with 20 ; the figures denoting the number of cents per pound for which the copper can be produced to whatever point on the earth's surface may represent the center of exchange, with reference to which prices are settled throughout the rest of the world.

Leaving out of consideration the confusions introduced by protective tariffs, it is easy to discover the general law under which these mines will be operated. If the price of copper at the center of exchange stand at 15, the mines represented by figures higher than 15 will remain unworked. If the price rise to 18, mines 19 and 20 only will stand idle. If it sink to 12, those above that figure will go unworked. The rise and fall of the price at the center of exchange will fix the line, on one side of which the mines can be profitably operated, while on the other side they can be worked only at a loss.

If the price stand at 15, and the owners of mines represented by 16 and 17 persist in operating them, the effect will of necessity be to force the price downward below 15 at the center of exchange. For a true price represents the point at which demand and supply are equal. If supply be increased price must fall to a point at which sufficient additional demand is created to absorb the additional sup-

ply. For the world is already using all the copper it can afford to
use at 15. There are industries that can use it to advantage at 14,
but to induce them to purchase the price must fall to that figure.
When the product of mines 16 and 17 is thrown upon the market
in addition to the product of the mines represented by 15 and
under, one of two things must follow. Either the price will fall or
the extra copper sent to market will remain unsold.

If the owners of all the mines below 17 agree together to force
the price from 15 up to 17 by the stmple expedient of refusing to
sell below 17, there is nothing to prevent them doing it. The thing
that they are not able to do is to compel the world to take at 17
the same quantity of copper that it would take at 15. The world
simply cannot do it. It cannot afford to do it. Industries that
flourish with copper at 15 will languish when copper rises to 16 and
perish utterly when it advances to 17. The law of supply and
demand is of nature's own ordaining. Human effort and human
legislation are powerless against it.

The copper syndicate thought otherwise. They imagined that
because this law of nature didn't please them they could change or
prevent its action by determined opposition. They actually believed that if they united all the copper mine owners under their
leadership, they would be able to compel the world to consume, at
17, the same amount of copper that it had been consuming at 15.
They didn't expect to succeed immediately. They were willing to
wait awhile, and fortified themselves for the period of waiting with
immense capital and credit. But they were fully satisfied that the
demand for copper at 15 represented the quantity which the world
absolutely needed and must have, even at a higher price. So having formed their combination of mine owners they fixed the price
of copper at the figure they thought proper, and settled themselves
to wait until the world should get through sulking and conclude to
come and buy.

Then it was grand to see how calmly and relentlessly the God-
made law of nature asserted itself. The syndicate twisted, turned,
wriggled, appealed—but nature kept on never minding. The artificial advance in the price of copper stimulated production as never
before. From every quarter of the globe mine owners rushed to
the enchanted spot where a pack of fools, with the coffers of a great
bank behind them, were paying for copper three, four, five, six

cents a pound more than it was worth. And the faster they came forward, the more the copper users held aloof. Supply was pushed one way, demand another. They got so far apart at last that even the resources of one of the greatest banks in Europe were insufficient to span the gulf between them. And then the great copper syndicate, with the great Bank of Discount at its back, fell with a resounding smash. It had tried to set nature at defiance, and nature just quietly knocked it into smithereens and went on about her business. And the result would have been just the same if the syndicate had had at its command the resources of the Bank of England and of the United States treasury to boot. For though a child may lead a horse to water, an army cannot make him drink. And though a syndicate of capitalists may prevent men using copper, a thousand syndicates, with all the treasuries of earth to strengthen them, cannot force men to buy as much copper at a high price as at a low one.

[From THE AMERICAN ECONOMIST, Aug. 16, 1889.]

INDUSTRIAL COMBINATION.

The views on this subject persistently advocated by the *American Economist* are gradually finding approval and support in many of the more prominent journals of the country. The Indianapolis *Journal*, the Albany *Journal*, and others of like character, do not hesitate to defend the advantages for the public welfare of the principle of combination. Other prominent journals have so far modified their views that they no longer attach such combinations indiscriminately, but confine their assaults to those which are manifestly hostile to public interests, and which deserve to be restrained in their operation by public opinion and the application of existing laws. .

The organ of the Federation of Labor plainly declares in favor of this principle as an illustration of the tendency of the age, and especially favorable to the condition of workingmen. The following, from an influential Democratic paper, expresses concurrence with our views in another form :

A LABOR TRUST.

Representatives of the American Federation of Labor, the Knights of Labor, the Brotherhood of Railroad Firemen, and the National Mutual Aid Association of Railroad Switchmen met in Philadelphia recently and conferred with regard to preventing hostilities and promoting union between the different labor organizations. A circular has been sent to officers of trades unions and district assemblies asking them to work for the programme of union, and calling "upon all unorganized workingmen to study the principles of organization, to meet and consult with members of labor societies in the various localities, with the object in view of ultimately bringing within the fold of labor organizations every worthy man and woman who toils in America."

The interesting thing about this project for a general union of the whole mass of labor in labor organizations is that it recognizes and follows the modern tendency toward the prevention of competition by consolidation. Could there be an organization of all the members of any given trade, it would be difficult to lower the wages of workers in that trade. There would be no others to supply their places. They would have a certain kind of skilled labor to sell, and they would control the market. They would continue to control it until their price became so high that there would be a great rush from abroad and a great development at home of that kind of labor. Then, unless the combination could control this new supply, it would break down. But it would be a Labor Trust. In unskilled labor the supply is so much greater that the difficulty of making a great combination or trust would be immensely increased; but the principle remains the same.

Now, a combination to put up the price of labor is, if successful, a useful thing for those who belong to it; but is just as essentially a trust as if sugar and not labor were the commodity which it aimed to control.

Let us call things, good or bad, by their true names. No humbug!